Of Different Minds

MAREN ANGELOTTI, M.A.T.

Of Different Minds

Seeing Your AD/HD Child
Through the Eyes of God

Regal

From Gospel Light
Ventura, California, U.S.A.

Published by Regal
From Gospel Light
Ventura, California, U.S.A.
www.regalbooks.com
Printed in the U.S.A.

Library of Congress Cataloging-in-Publication Data
Angelotti, Maren.
Of different minds : seeing your AD/HD child through the eyes of God / Maren
Angelotti.
p. cm.
Includes bibliographical references.
ISBN 978-0-8307-4720-7 (trade paper)
1. Attention-deficit-disordered children. 2. Attention-deficit hyperactivity disorder—
Religious aspects—Christianity. 3. Problem children—Behavior modification. 4.
Parenting. I. Title.
RJ506.H9A5954 2008
618.92'8589—dc22
2008040848

1 2 3 4 5 6 7 8 9 10 / 15 14 13 12 11 10 09

Rights for publishing this book outside the U.S.A. or in non-English languages are administered by Gospel Light Worldwide, an international not-for-profit ministry. For additional information, please visit www.glww.org, email info@glww.org, or write to Gospel Light Worldwide, 1957 Eastman Avenue, Ventura, CA 93003, U.S.A.

I dedicate this book to my four children—
Christopher, Jaclyn, Nicholas and Alicia—who have
brought me tremendous joy.
Thank you for sharing your learning differences with the world.
You are my heroes. Remember, you are loved!

Contents

Resources

Acknowledgments

I want to acknowledge several special people in my life. First and foremost, my beloved husband, Bob, whose humor, constant love and Christ-like spirit keep us all centered. To my parents, Charles J. Chodzko, Jr. (Papa) and Mary T. Chodzko (Gommie), whose constant support and encouragement have been invaluable to us throughout the years—you mean the world to your children, 15 grandchildren and 5 great-grandchildren.

I would also like to thank my colleagues: Gayle Chilcoat, M.Ed., CALT, whose insight and love of the learning-different population never ceases. Janet Arnold, Ph.D., a gifted and talented learning specialist who truly cares about learning-different people, for her diligence and hard work in making me understand the true meaning of "ADD." Suzanne Stell, M.Ed., CALT and Head of School for the Shelton School, who took the time and wisdom to see the gifts of my children—thank you for being there from the start and guiding us to the finish line. Joyce Pickering, Hum.D., CCC-SLP, CALT, QI, and Executive Director of the Shelton School, whose invaluable research, inspired by her genuine love for this population, will contribute to fulfilling futures for learning-different students—thank you for believing not only in my children's success but in my own, and for being an incredible mentor and valued friend. To the entire Shelton community—thank you for your dedication to and love of learning-different individuals. I am honored to know all of you. You have inspired me to do what I do on a daily basis. Thank you for being part of my life.

I would also like to acknowledge Dr. Daniel Amen, M.D., Medical Director and CEO of the Amen Clinics. Your outstanding research and dedication to uncovering the mysteries of the AD/HD mind will forever change the way learning differences are perceived. I appreciate your kind words of encouragement on this project. And to Dr. Todd Clements, M.D.—thank you for your constant encouragement and education on the SPECT imaging for this project. My family is forever in your debt. It has been an honor to work with you.

To all my students, past and present, that continue to humble me—thank you for allowing me into your moments of struggle. You never give up, even when the going gets tough. You always see the deeper vision of what could be, and you are not afraid to make it a reality. You are the ones who will change the world.

Above all, I want to express my eternal gratitude to Almighty God, the Creator, who is forever faithful. By Him and in His image, each person is "wonderfully made" and given a mind in which to know Him and His unending love.

My Story

"She just doesn't stay on task."

"She is not working up to her potential."

"We know that she is very bright, but she just appears lazy."

"He doesn't turn his homework in on time. Could you please make sure that he is doing it at home?"

"He talks and talks and talks. That's why his name is on the board every day."

"She always seems so worried. Is there something going on at home?"

I am the mother of four unique and wonderful children. I heard phrases like the ones above for years, and they defined three of my children throughout their early educational careers. Two of them were diagnosed with ADD, dyslexia and related disorders by the time they had reached fourth grade. Our youngest was diagnosed with auditory processing disorder and ADD at the end of her freshman year of high school.

Both my husband and I have learning differences as well; I have dyslexia and Bob has ADD. Our children had very little chance to escape these differences—they are hereditary—so our family has chosen to embrace them, to learn from them and to try to change the world through them. My husband has a wonderful sense of humor, and that has been the saving grace many times on our journey.

Bob and I decided that I would be a stay-at-home mom. I was thrilled about this decision when I was about eight-and-a-half months pregnant with Chris, our firstborn; I was so excited at the prospect of being there at every stage of his life, watching him grow up. After Chris was about four months old, however, I was bored and incredibly lonely. The transition was very difficult. I had had a good job with a bank and loved being on the go all the time, and suddenly I was on call for this baby who slept around the clock. None of our friends were having babies yet, so there was no one to talk to during the day. I could see why so many women in our society want to return to their jobs at the sixth-month mark, but I could also see that going back to work so soon would be selfish.

I kept plugging on until Chris was about six or seven months old, and it was then I realized that the early months of motherhood were a time to prepare myself for raising God's child. Instead of being bored and lonely, I had a chance to quiet myself and listen to God in my prayer time, asking Him how to parent this child. I realized that it was not about me anymore; it was about me giving myself totally to someone else. I thought I had done this when I married, but this level of selfless giving was something new altogether.

The boredom and loneliness that seemed to overpower me in the early days gave way to a new kind of busy when I became pregnant again only eight months after Chris was born. My pregnancy with Jackie made me want to spend as much time as possible with Chris, and our alone-time together laid an important foundation that time at a daycare center never could. Little did I know that my early decision to choose staying at home over myself would prepare me to raise four wonderful children, three of whom were challenged by learning differences.

The truth is, another person cannot love our children the way we do. I encourage parents to scrutinize their situations fearlessly and honestly to determine whether or not they are leaving their child out of true necessity. Take time to become the parents God intended; it will surpass any job you leave behind or put on hold. The days may seem tedious sometimes, but when each day is stitched together over the years, they make the most beautiful tapestry of a little soul.

> Take time to become the parents God intended; it will surpass any job you leave behind or put on hold.

Chris was an easy child to raise. He always wanted to please. When asked to watch out for his brother and sisters, he usually did a great job because he was very intuitive about his siblings. He may not have understood their learning differences, but he did know how to help them understand life situations. One such situation happened when my husband was driving the kids one blustery winter afternoon to meet me at a church function. The roads were icy and the three youngest children were being kids, laughing and carrying on in the back seat. Chris was up front in the passenger side when Bob, my husband, spun out on the ice, doing a complete 360. Chris turned around to the back seat and said very calmly, "Everyone be quiet. This is important. We are having an accident. Hold on to each other, please." The car came to a complete stop in the middle of the freeway. When he saw that no other cars were around, Chris asked Bob, "What are we supposed to do now?" Chris always watched out for his brother and sisters.

That doesn't mean that being a big brother to his learning-different siblings hasn't been a challenge for Chris; his patience has often been tried by their literal understanding of the world. I can see now that we did not always give him the tools he needed to help him understand his siblings. There were times when Chris would make a new friend only to have one of the other children say something embarrassing; sometimes the friend did not come back. I also think there were times when Chris felt lost and forgotten because Bob and I spent so much time helping the other kids deal with their difficulties. He appeared to have everything under control, which gave us the freedom to attend to the others. It was not until his high school years that we began to understand how deep his pain and resentment had become. He really felt he needed to separate himself from his brother and sisters to create healthy friendships with others. We respected that and tried to show the other children that he needed some space. As the years have progressed, their relationships have gotten much closer, and I believe that their bond will only grow deeper as their life journeys continue.

As of this writing, Chris is 24 and works for a prominent computer company. At the age of 16, he knew that he wanted to be the head of worldwide marketing for this company, and he asked to be homeschooled. When I asked why, he answered, "Because I know what I want to do. I want to get on with life." During his homeschool tenure, he began to sell the company's product at a local electronics retail store, and before long he had more than doubled their monthly sales. This caught the attention of the corporate headquarters, and at the age of 17, Chris was asked to create new venues for their product. Upon completing his communications degree from Loyola Marymount University, he began working in the marketing department and now travels internationally. Chris found his passion at a young age, and the sky is the limit for his dreams.

Our second child, Jackie, was a difficult infant, but when she turned four it was like a switch came on to show me a totally different child. As an infant, she did not like to be cuddled inwardly (for example, with her head on my chest); she always had to be facing out to see what was going on around her. She cried unless she was moving, whether it was rocking in the rocking chair or riding in the car. The only other thing that would soothe her was music; if I sang to her, she immediately calmed down. She also had terrible night terrors. She would wake up screaming, and the only thing to calm her was music or rocking. Later, I came to understand that she had some sensory integration challenges. ("Sensory integration is the neurological process of organizing the information we get from our bodies and from the world around us for use in daily life."[1]) God created Jackie's nerve endings very close to the surface of her skin, so every time I held her too close, her skin was irritated. (I thought that I was just a terrible mother and that my daughter couldn't bond with me.) When she wore shirts or pants with tags in the backs of them, she went through the roof until I removed them.

Yet when Jackie turned four years old, she became quite calm. She retreated into a world of make-believe. It was precious to watch her play with her dolls, but odd that she named every doll or playmate Sally. Chris was only 18 months older than Jackie, and they played together all the time. Chris created elaborate games, such as "Bank." It would take him forever to set his room up like a bank, and by then Jackie's attention would have switched gears to play quietly with "Sally."

Jackie is now in her last semester of college. She will graduate with a degree in Communications for Film and TV with minors in Journalism and in Theater. She attends Eckerd College in Florida and has loved every minute of it. As of this writing, she is an intern with a prominent national news network and hopes to work with them full time upon graduation. Jackie was diagnosed with ADD (the inattentive type), dyslexia and dyscalculia (we'll discuss these in detail in chapter 1). The Lord gave her tremendous gifts of music; she has a voice that won't quit! She has sung on projects for Disney as well as backup vocals for several popular artists. She is also a lyricist and has shared her own music in many venues. During her early years, teachers told me that Jackie would never attend college and that I'd better help her learn a trade. Little did they know . . .

Nicholas, our third child, came into the world on Easter Sunday as a 10-pound baby, screaming his lungs out; he has not stopped letting us know that he has something to say from that moment since. He, like the others, has been a blast to raise, but during his toddler years I might not have said so. Nick followed the two older kids around, wanting to play with them, but he is four years younger than Chris (which is a big difference during the early years). When he couldn't find them or was not included, he found adventures of his own. One year, Nick dressed up as a pirate for Halloween. We made a sword out of foil for him, and he thought it was the greatest weapon in the world. When the others wouldn't play with him, he dressed up in the pirate outfit, waited for the neighbor to come out to get his morning paper, and then poked him in the behind and warned, "You better be nicer to the kids on the block, mister!" Needless to say, I was always over at the neighbor's house apologizing.

Bedtime for Nick was a huge battle. Had I known then what I know now, his daytime and bedtime routines would have looked very different. I used to take my kids every day to explore the world; I didn't know that too much stimuli for a child with ADD is like a time bomb ready to explode in their brains. They need routine, routine, routine, and a very calm environment. When bedtime rolled around, the time bomb exploded in outrageous temper tantrums. These tantrums could occur on our outings as well. I attributed Nick's outbursts to normal behavior for a toddler, but his lasted until he was about nine years old.

Both Jackie and Nick kept us entertained when we went on family drives up the coast to Santa Barbara. When they were both toddlers, they had a terrible habit of using unusual words for common words. Nick would always preface words with "ba" or "mo." For example, he would say, "Hey, Mommy, close the ba-garage" or "There goes the mo-police." Jackie would look out at the ocean and say, "Look at the lotion, Mommy." These phrases and many more kept us in stitches, but they were indicators for future learning differences. As the years went on, Nick made *A*s and *B*s in school, but something stood out during the summer after his fourth-grade year. He had a reading list to complete, and as I sat listening to him read, I realized that he couldn't read well at all. I knew that something was going on, but what?

Nick was diagnosed with dyslexia and ADD when he was entering the fifth grade. He is now completing his sophomore year at Loyola Marymount University and plans for his last two years to attend Franklin College in Switzerland to study international business. He would like to work in Europe as a marketing executive with a soccer team. As an adult, he has never met a stranger and truly enjoys people. When asked how he feels about his learning difference, he says, "I love it. I don't know what the big deal is. Learning-different people aren't boring. We have a blast and we never take life for granted." Because he did so well in high school, he did not receive any accommodations for his learning differences in college. This has been a real challenge for him, but he has been able to keep his GPA up with the help of The Shelton School here in Dallas. This foundation offers him proper remediation for his dyslexia, direct teaching of social skills, small class size to meet the needs of those with impulsive ADD, and most importantly, the skills to be his own educational advocate. Nick now knows how he learns best and knows how to succeed.

Last but not least, our youngest, Alicia, was the easiest baby in the world. She was adorable. Jackie, who is seven years older, treated Alicia like her own personal doll. When the others went off to school, Alicia loved to line up all the crayons in a perfect row on the floor. She loved her alone-time with me and we would spend many wonderful days together at the beach, exploring marine life. When she entered school, she loved the structure and the rules, and was always anxious that she wasn't getting everything right. When she had me review her material for school tests, she fell apart if she missed even one answer.

Occasionally, she decided that I didn't know how to help her study, and that it was my fault if she didn't get her desired grade. I just attributed her reaction to perfectionism, the same impulse that prompted her to line up those crayons.

Alicia was an *A* and *B* student all through her early academic career, and it wasn't until she reached her freshman year of high school that we recognized that she too was struggling with a learning difference. She was diagnosed with ADD and auditory processing disorder—she only understood 4 percent of what she heard in the classroom. Can you imagine understanding only 4 percent of what's going on and being told that there will be a test on the material tomorrow? Talk about anxiety! It's the come-to-life version of that dream where you know you haven't been to class all semester and your college professor announces that the final exam is tomorrow . . . and then you wake up in a cold sweat. Alicia was living it on a day-to-day basis. Once her situation was clear to us, we immediately transferred her to The Shelton School in hopes that she would have the same positive experience as Nick. We did not hope in vain: Alicia is doing beautifully now, looking forward to college and a degree in journalism. She has discovered that her gifts are in writing—both poetry and fiction—and she also loves design of all types. It will be a joy to watch her future unfold.

* * *

It is important to me to start my story and this book with the successes achieved by these remarkable people, which have been attained through trials great, small and many. But I must confess that while I am now confident that my children's learning differences will never stand in the way of their dreams, early on I was a parent in denial. When teachers told me that my children were showing signs of ADD or dyslexia, I was convinced that they didn't know what they were talking about. After all, I knew my children better than they did! None of my children had any of "those problems."

I wish I had known then what I know now: *God has a special purpose in mind for every person created in His image, and that includes each one who is learning-different!* Three of my children live in the world of learning differences, and today they are succeeding and sharing their unique, God-given gifts in a tremendous way. But helping them deal with their challenges and guiding them through life has not always been easy. Throughout this book, I will share more of our family's story. I hope you'll see that living with learning differences can draw your family closer together and teach you things you have never imagined.

> God has a special purpose in mind for every person created in His image, and that includes each one who is learning-different!

After Chris, our oldest, graduated from high school, I decided to learn more about learning differences. I began to take classes, and almost before I knew it I had completed my master's degree in Teaching for the Multisensory Child. I now had an effective combination of personal and educational experiences, and it was my goal to use these to build up the kingdom of God, one child or adult at a time.

I have written this book to encourage and educate parents as they begin or continue their journey down a winding road. There are so many who have gone before who have given me the courage to go on day by day. Other mothers and fathers have shown me the wisdom and the patience needed to raise three of these incredible people. Outstanding educators have dissolved my misunderstandings about learning differences and given me the foundation and tools to guide my children toward success and satisfaction. Inspired by their encouragement, examples and influence, I hope to extend what I have learned to those who come after me through these pages.

THE EDISON GENE

Learning differences have been with us since time began. Thom Hartmann, author of *The Edison Gene: ADHD and the Gift of the Hunter Child* and *Attention-Deficit Disorder: A Different Perception*, suggests that our primitive ancestors depended on the skills of individuals who were able to hunt and gather for the group.[2] Hartmann also contends that these individuals possessed the traits of our AD/HD population today. They were not afraid to take risks; they scanned the horizon (literally and figuratively) for new environments that were beneficial for their group. As time progressed, these same types of individuals explored new worlds and encountered new cultures, bringing new and transforming ideas from one civilization to another.

Thom Hartmann writes:

What exactly defines those bearing this genetic makeup? Edison-gene children and adults are by nature:

Enthusiastic

Creative

Disorganized

Non-linear in their thinking (they leap to new conclusions or observations)

Innovative

Easily distracted (or, to put it differently, easily attracted to new stimuli)

Capable of extraordinary hyper-focus

Understanding of what it means to be an "outsider"

Determined

Eccentric

Easily bored

Impulsive

Entrepreneurial

Energetic

All of these qualities lead them to be natural:

Explorers

Inventors

Discoverers

Leaders

Those carrying this gene, however, often find them-selves in environments where they're coerced, threat-ened, or shoehorned into a classroom or job that doesn't fit. When Edison-gene children aren't recognized for their gifts but instead are told that they're disordered, broken, or failures, a great emotional and spiritual wounding occurs. This wounding can bring about all sorts of problems for children, for the adults they grow into, and for our society.[3]

Today, these hunter-gatherer individuals are not as valued within our culture as they were thousands of years ago. Instead, we tend to value people who are detailed in their thinking and able to learn in a rote environment. In agrarian societies, long before our technological age, these individuals were the workers—they loved to do the same thing over and over—who implemented the grand ideas of the hunter-gatherers.

God created both types of people, and human societies (ancient *and* modern) work best when both types are valued, honored and respected. Let me give you a few examples of modern-day hunter-gatherers who have literally changed our world.

Thomas Edison was one of the most prolific inventors in history, holding a record 1,093 U.S. patents. He gave us the light bulb, the movie projector and the phonograph. Without him, where would we be today? (I'm betting we'd still be in the dark!) When Edison's third-grade teacher reprimanded him for being inattentive, fidgety and "slow," Thomas's mother, Nancy Edison (the well-educated daughter of a Presbyterian minister), was deeply offended by the schoolmaster's characterization of her son. She pulled Thomas out of the school and became his teacher, until the day he went off to work for the railroads (inventing, in his first months of employment, a railroad timing and signaling device that was used for nearly a century). Nancy believed in her son and she refused to let the school thrash out of him his belief in himself. As a result of one mother's efforts, the world is a very different place.[4]

Charles R. Schwab also overcame the odds. As a schoolboy, he struggled with reading and coped by immersing himself in *Classic* comic books, which he could understand because of the pictures. His parents, by all accounts, felt that Charles would grow out of it and so ignored the problem. Without their help, his struggle was long and embarrassing. Thankfully, Charles had strong social traits; he made friends easily and instinctively played on his strengths in science and math to succeed in school. Charles was not aware that he suffered from dyslexia until his own child was diagnosed with it, and from that time forward, he has contributed millions of dollars to help parents understand and cope with their children's learning differences through the All Kinds of Minds Institute.[5]

Paul Orfalea, the founder of Kinko's, has often said, "After graduation, the A students work for the B students, the C students run the companies, and the D students dedicate the buildings."[6] As a language therapist for learning-different children, I find this often to be true. Our world believes that you must be an A student at all costs, but intelligence is not measured by grades. If a student is working to their full potential in the classroom and is making Bs, Cs or even Ds, don't sell them short—given the right motivation and opportunity, they may out-imagine, out-invent and out-achieve their classmates. Thomas Edison, Charles Schwab and Paul Orfalea all used their strengths to change the world for the better—and your learning-different child can, too!

It is my hope that this book—full of stories about real children, teens, adults and families learning to survive and thrive with learning differences, as well as case studies from my own practice and the latest scientific findings—will empower you to do more than cope with your child's learning difference. Our society needs your child's unique perspective on and perception of the world as we move further into the twenty-first century. I pray that *Of Different Minds* will give you the tools you need to help your precious gift from God flourish and grow into all he or she is created to be.

SECTION ONE

THE WHAT AND WHY OF LEARNING DIFFERENCES

I

What Are Learning
Differences?

The National Center for Learning Disabilities defines a learning disability as "a neurological disorder that affects the brain's ability to receive, process, store and respond to information."[1] Individuals with learning disabilities are generally of average or above-average intelligence, but there is a gap between their cognitive ability and their performance.

Learning disabilities (or "differences," as many educators prefer to call them, to emphasize very real potential rather than problems) are hereditary. Many times, parents with learning-different children are learning-different themselves, but have never had a formal diagnosis. When they hear a diagnostician describe their child's behaviors, thought processes and challenges, a light goes on: They remember going through a very similar thing when they were children. And even if they do not share ADD, AD/HD, dyslexia or another learning difference with their child, most look back far enough in their family tree to find a brother or sister (or perhaps their wacky Uncle Harry) who carry the genetic traits.

PROBLEMS IN SCHOOL

There are eight major causes of problems in school, and it is easy to mistake a perceptual dysfunction (that is, a learning disability) for some other problem. Before we look at some specific learning differences, let's define what learning differences are *not*.

The eight major causes of school difficulties are:

1. Sensory Deprivation

Sensory deprivation, which occurs when children do not receive proper stimuli in infancy and through their earliest years, is not a learning difference. Cuddling and verbal interaction are necessary in the natural progression of human development, and when they are withheld, children are often impaired mentally, emotionally and socially. Sensory deprivation is typically found in orphanages and some daycare centers where children are left for long hours without any tactical stimuli. These extreme conditions have been proven to make a detrimental impact on the learning process later in life.

Orphanages in developing countries are often filled with children who lie in their cribs for days on end with no human contact. I know a family who adopted a four-year-old child from Romania. They went to visit her there several times over the two years it took to finalize her adoption. When the day finally arrived for their family to be united, their eyes filled with happy tears.

Unfortunately, as the years rolled on, those tears were replaced with fear. The little girl could not seem to bond with her adoptive parents, and she had great difficulty relating properly with teachers and classmates. She would go to the corner of the playground to avoid being social with the other children. If she was coaxed into being around other kids, before long she would push them or start fights.

While this little girl's behavior may have appeared, at first glance, to indicate ADD or AD/HD, her difficulties were a result of sensory deprivation, not of a learning difference. In order for her to thrive in her new family and environment, she needed intensive and specialized treatment.

2. Cultural Deprivation or Disadvantage

Cultural deprivation, which occurs when children are not exposed to experiences and stimuli that prepare them for education, is not a learning difference. Most sociologists and educators agree that if young children are not given an early opportunity to begin their learning adventure, they will face challenges throughout their school years. This very early education demands a high level of parent involvement, but in our society it is common for parents to use the TV as a babysitter instead of engaging their young child in activities that prepare him or her for education, such as reading books aloud, coloring, playing with shapes and numbers, listening to and making music, and so on.

Likewise, in many daycares, it is not rare to find children staring at a TV screen instead of being engaged by their caregivers. Unfortunately, many of these caregivers are not educated themselves about how to stimulate the minds of young children toward effective learning for the future. Could this be one of the reasons that our public education system has lowered the bar of learning? Could this be one of the reasons that students in the United States are having trouble competing with other regions in the world?

3. Educational Deficiency

Unfortunately, educational deficiency is a widespread problem. It is most common in communities that are socio-economically disadvantaged, whether here in the U.S. or in developing countries with little or no resources for education. Educational deficiency is exactly what it sounds like: a lack of academic opportunity among children who are otherwise capable of attending and achieving in school. It is not a learning difference.

I can't help but think of "the lost boys of Sudan," 27,000 boys who were displaced after the second Sudanese Civil War (1984-2005). Thirty-eight hundred of them arrived in the United States in 2001 and are scattered throughout 38 states. I had the opportunity to work with one such boy here in the Dallas area. Dahar was his given name, but he changed it to John so that the other kids would not make fun of him.

> Educational deficiency is a lack of academic opportunity among children who are otherwise capable of attending and achieving in school.

Because of the war and extreme poverty in his homeland, John had not regularly attended school at any time in his life. And even though he was extremely bright and eager to learn, soaking up everything about his new surroundings, he lagged very far behind others of the same age.

4. Low Mental Ability

IQ, which stands for "intelligence quotient," is a very important measure of how an individual perceives and understands the world around them. IQ does matter. With an average to above-average IQ, your child has a better chance to succeed in his or her education. Yet for some reason, we sometimes hear from the media and even from so-called educational experts that IQ does not determine what a child will do with his or her future. This may be true for a very few, but not for the majority of us.

The following is a typical IQ scale:

Above 130	=	Very superior
120-129	=	Superior
110-119	=	High average
90-109	=	Average
80-90	=	Low average
70-79	=	Borderline
Below 69	=	Intellectually deficit

I have found that some schools do not regard IQ evaluation as necessary when accepting learning-different students. I believe this is unfair to the learning-different community, who generally have high cognitive ability. When IQ is not taken into account, schools sometimes lump learning-different students together with students who are mentally retarded, autistic or who suffer from Asperger syndrome. In this scenario, those with learning differences usually do not receive adequate remediation and social-skills training, and often have difficulty achieving to their high potential.

5. Mental Retardation
People with IQs below 70 are clinically categorized as mentally retarded. Retardation is not a learning difference.

The Caldwell family had four children. The youngest son, Kevin, was diagnosed as mentally retarded when he was four years old. Although the Caldwells were distressed at Kevin's diagnosis, they worked with the public school system (which has a good record of helping this population) to accommodate his educational needs. Kevin graduated from high school when he was 23 and learned a trade. He lives in a group home and loves his job at the YMCA. He is a complete joy to be around.

Through the years, Kevin's parents have worked together as a team to help him become the best he can be. With the help of educational accommodations, they raised a son who is a blessing to all who know him.

6. Frank Brain Damage

People who have sustained sudden injury to the brain may exhibit behaviors similar to those who are AD/HD, but brain damage is not a learning difference. The areas of the brain affected by learning differences may be damaged by trauma, which can result in behavior that mimics AD/HD or a related disorder. If this is the case with your child, he or she may benefit from classes or schools designed with learning-different students in mind.

I had a dear friend whose child was in an auto accident. She was in a coma for several days after the crash. When she awoke, she had to learn how to walk and talk again, and it took her nearly two years and countless hours in rehab to recover. Her tenacity was an inspiration to everyone, but even after two years, her doctors told her that she would always have difficulty with short-term memory and detail work, which are typical traits of learning-different students.

Coping with the changes and challenges resulting from brain damage can be a difficult adjustment. Rehab, retraining and remediation can be a long and sometimes disappointing journey, especially if the person feels that he or she should be capable of more. Given the right treatment and environment, however, a person with brain trauma can often activate areas of his or her brain that are undamaged, relearning physical, cognitive and social function.

7. Primary Emotional Problems

Emotional problems are among the most prevalent challenges we face as a society today, and children are just as susceptible to depression, anxiety and other problems as adults. Divorce and other family dysfunctions put enormous pressure on a child's emotions, which can have a negative effect on his or her learning experience.

> How can we expect a child to learn successfully when there is no family foundation to make them feel secure enough to explore the world outside the home?

I recently had a student come in for therapy. He was having a difficult time concentrating on our conversation and exercises, and that's when I noticed huge tears rolling down his face. When I asked him what was the matter, he said, "My mom said she and my dad are getting a divorce. I'm only seven. How can this happen to me?"

Divorce, one of the most common causes of emotional distress in children's lives, has become a national epidemic, and the fallout is that children are disconnected from their families and their communities. And while emotional problems are not learning differences, how can we expect a child to learn successfully when there is no family foundation to make them feel secure enough to explore the world outside the home? Our society is facing a grave danger; parents must put their children's wellbeing above their own needs and desires so that kids grow up strong, healthy and ready for life.

8. Perceptual Dysfunction

Perceptual dysfunctions *are* learning differences, and these can be a challenge for students trying to succeed in school. *Throughout this book, we will be exploring and addressing perceptual dysfunctions.*

Students with perceptual dysfunctions have difficulty with visual memory, visual discrimination, motor function, auditory discrimination, auditory memory or a combination of these.

An example of visual memory dysfunction is difficulty copying from the board, while an example of visual discrimination disability is confusing the letters *b* and *d*, *p* and *q*, *m* and *w*, *n* and *u*. Motor function difficulties include problems with dictation and written expression, while perceptual errors in auditory discrimination manifest as difficulty hearing and understanding words (for example, a student with auditory discrimination might hear "wisp" when someone says "whisk," "smug" instead of "snug," "deaf" rather than "death" or "lotion" instead of "ocean"). This can lead to poor comprehension when following directions and taking notes. A person with auditory memory problems has difficulty remembering conversations and instructions, which also makes following directions difficult.

It is important for parents to get good and accurate testing to make sure they know what learning difference(s) their child is dealing with. Learning differences can be dyslexia, ADD, AD/HD or a related disorder. (We will discuss related disorders later.) Once they have gotten the diagnosis, it is imperative that they understand what all of the terms mean. So here we go!

WHAT IS AD/HD?

AD/HD is an executive function problem that affects learning and sometimes social skills. ("Executive function" refers to an overarching cognitive process that controls other cognitive processes, such as planning, abstract thinking, inhibiting inappropriate behaviors and selecting relevant information.) ADD means Attention-Deficit Disorder without hyperactive behavior, but distractibility is a prime characteristic. In a classroom, the ADD student can stay in his chair but constantly misses information because he cannot focus or concentrate normally. ADHD is all this along with hyperactivity. It is common to refer to ADD and ADHD together as AD/HD.

Persons who have ADD and AD/HD generally have normal or above IQ levels. The ADD child's attention, focus and concentration are erratic. She is with you and then she's not. She seems to be daydreaming. Many of these children are quiet and go from grade to grade being unnoticed by the teacher. A child with AD/HD, on the other hand, may be described by teachers as "extremely wiggly." His parents may be told that he is never still in school; he is rarely at rest in any situation. His hyperactivity can be noted almost from birth; he frequently has sleep and feeding problems as a baby. He is into everything as a preschooler. Under stress, he may fall apart completely. He can have temper tantrums and is often described as impatient.

In school, children with AD/HD have difficulty with reading comprehension, math, writing and spelling. Their writing is usually very poor and their spelling is often inaccurate. They are described as very distractible. Actually, they *are* attending, but they are attending to every incoming sensory stimuli in their surroundings. They cannot ignore the less important sights and sounds in their environment to focus their attention on the most important information. For example, a student may detect her teacher giving directions and notice a butterfly landing on a bush outside the window and see her neighbor pulling out a piece of paper from his binder, all with the same intensity.

> Children with AD/HD cannot ignore the less important sights and sounds in their environment to focus their attention on the most important information.

Violet was a student of mine who shared many of these traits. Every time we began our lesson, she had to tell me everything on her mind. She lacked the ability to know when it was appropriate to speak and when not to speak. It was as if the floodgates of information flowed at full speed all the time and could not be stopped until everything was out. It amazes me how the unremediated mind can move as quickly as it does. As a therapist, I tried to redirect Violet to the work at hand by guiding her with social cues, or by simply pointing to the work for that session. AD/HD children need a lot of reassurance and encouragement to find their world safe enough for learning to occur.

Working with Violet, I could tell that one moment she was with me and the next she was not. Her facial expression would indicate that she did not understand the directions and she looked very lost. Even after I repeated the directions two more times, she still seemed confused. It was only when I asked her to repeat what I had said that she began to register what was going on in her surroundings.

Reading (decoding) may or may not be affected in the child with AD/HD. Many times, the student with AD/HD can "read" words, but does not comprehend what he has read. This is due to the fact that the student's focus shifts as he is reading, which causes word meaning to simply dissolve from his short-term memory.

I currently have a student that can read anything that is put in front of him, but he does not comprehend anything he reads. Through his remediation process, which has been very long and tedious, he is just now able to put meaning to language. This particular student has benefited greatly from a speech therapist, who dissects language used in his everyday world, and a language therapist. The language therapist helps this student to paraphrase what he reads, which improves his comprehension.

Not every AD/HD student has reading difficulty this severe, but it does happen. The important thing is to address it as soon as possible, while the brain is still elastic enough to change its wiring. Recent research indicates that remediation processes actually change the white matter of the brain.[2] This is great news. We now know that we can bring educational success for life. What a great gift to the next generation!

Almost all AD/HD students have writing difficulties, characterized by poor slant, poor spacing, and omitted or added letters and words. Their writing gets worse the longer they write. With training they can improve their writing skills, but they rarely have excellent handwriting even after remediation. In this day and age of computers, most people don't even bother with writing things by hand; they usually send emails or text messages. But, believe it or not, it is very important for a learning-different student to learn cursive and learn it at a very young age. The fluid motion of writing cursive actually stimulates the learning-different part of the brain.[3] I recommend that students master cursive before they move to learning the keyboard. Typically, fifth grade is a good time for a learning-different student to learn keyboarding. I know that this sounds crazy in our technological world, but not everything technological is always the best way.

AD/HD students' math skills are sometimes poor due to their problems with writing and spelling, which affect most subjects at school. They may also have a more acute math difficulty, called dyscalculia (which we will explore later). It is very important for the AD/HD population to use tactile objects, called "manipulatives," when learning mathematical skills. These help students make abstract concepts concrete. In traditional classrooms, teachers may use manipulatives during the primary grades and then disregard them as infantile for older children. What a shame, because learning-different children need them to master an understanding of the logical world of math. The action of moving objects into various configurations again and again helps them to establish mathematical relationships. When concrete relationships are firmly in place, then they are able to conceptualize abstract relationships without using manipulatives.

The person with an Attention-Deficit Disorder often has marked problems with motor skills and may have poor balance. She can achieve in sports, but she has to work at the skills she wants to master. She often will not compete with other girls and boys her own age, preferring to play with younger or older girls and boys so that she is not required to compete on an equal footing. Most learning-different children and adults are very competitive, due to their constant struggle to keep up with their peers. This is not necessarily a bad thing. Their competitive spirit can be to their advantage in their chosen career someday.

Six Types of AD/HD

It is imperative for parents to have a working knowledge of AD/HD and the comorbidity (two or more learning differences existing together) that can come along with it. The Amen Clinic, founded by Dr. Daniel G. Amen, has pioneered the use of SPECT (Single Photo Emission Computed Tomography) imaging to give us a more intimate look at the AD/HD brain. His research has proven invaluable to thousands seeking to understand their difficulties. Dr. Amen has classified ADD into six types to help the average person understand his scans of ADD more clearly, and his book, *Healing ADD: The Breakthrough Program that Allows You to See and Heal the 6 Types of ADD*, gives the most clear and concise understanding of ADD and its various complications.[4]

The six types of ADD are as follows:

TYPE 1: CLASSIC ADD
Sufferers are inattentive, distractible, disorganized, hyperactive, restless and impulsive.

TYPE 2: INATTENTIVE ADD
Sufferers are inattentive, sluggish, slow-moving, have low motivation and are often described as "space cadets," "daydreamers" or "couch potatoes."

TYPE 3: OVERFOCUSED ADD
Sufferers have trouble shifting attention; frequently get stuck in loops of negative thoughts or behaviors; are obsessive; worry excessively; are inflexible; and frequently behave oppositionally and argumentatively.

TYPE 4: TEMPORAL LOBE ADD
Sufferers are inattentive, irritable, aggressive, have dark thoughts and mood instability, and are severely impulsive.

TYPE 5: LYMBIC ADD
Sufferers are inattentive, experience chronic low-grade depression, are negative, have low energy and frequent feelings of hopelessness and worthlessness.

TYPE 6: RING OF FIRE ADD
Sufferers are inattentive, extremely distractible, angry, irritable, overly sensitive to the environment, hyperverbal, extremely oppositional and experience cyclical mood.

The Amen Clinic has graciously allowed me to share with you several scans to give you a clearer perspective of ADD and what it looks like at work in the brain. Below are some SPECT scans of various brain behaviors. See for yourself what learning differences look like through the eyes of modern technology.

Scan 1 is that of a healthy brain with no signs of ADD or the related disorders.

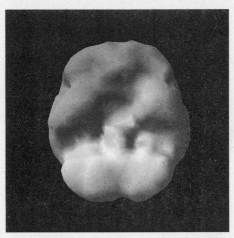

SCAN 1 (Courtesy of the Amen Clinic, Newport Beach, California)

Scan 2 on the following page is of a female age 34 who has ADD. The first view is seen from under the brain. Moving to the right is a view looking at the right side of the brain. The lower left view is looking at the left side of the brain. The final view is from the top looking down. The areas that look like holes are actually areas of the brain that lack cerebral blood flow. Basically, the brain is not fully activated within these areas. As you can see, her brain is under-activated, not firing up for her to be able to work to her potential.

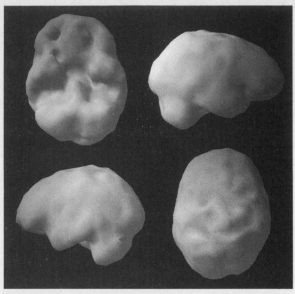

SCAN 2 (Courtesy of the Amen Clinic, Newport Beach, California)

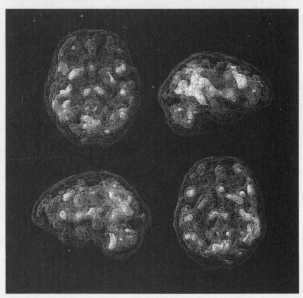

SCAN 3 (Courtesy of the Amen Clinic, Newport Beach, California)

Next is Scan 3, which is of an 11-year old girl with Ring of Fire ADD as described by Dr. Amen. As you can see, the areas in white are firing up too hot, which causes the girl to be extremely irritable and easily distracted. She is prone to cyclical moods and shows many oppositional traits. She needs the white areas of her brain to cool down before she can learn. Her parents did not know the severity of her situation until they had this scan. Her father was in denial. He thought that she would just outgrow her difficulties. Once he was able to see these scans, however, he was more open to the proper therapies to bring about success for his child.

Scan 4 is a normal brain of a female age 8-14. As you can see, this is a shocking contrast from the young girl above. The

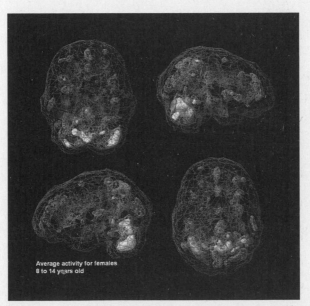

Average activity for females
8 to 14 years old

SCAN 4 (Courtesy of the Amen Clinic, Newport Beach, California)

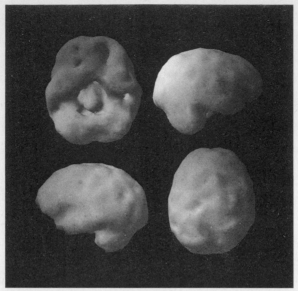

SCAN 5 (Courtesy of the Amen Clinic, Newport Beach, California)

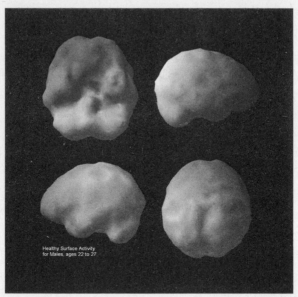

SCAN 6 (Courtesy of the Amen Clinic, Newport Beach, California)

white area in this scan is the cerebellum, which controls balance, motor skills and coordination. This area should always show up as white.

Scan 5 shows a male age 23 who suffers from ADD and violence. Often, individuals with violent temperaments have had some sort of brain injury. One common thread is those who have played football; they have been knocked around so much that they don't know that they have a brain injury. You can see the brain injury in the left temporal lobe when you compare Scan 5 with Scan 6, which is of a healthy 23-year-old male.

Scan 7 on the following page is of a 17-year-old male with ADD and other learning differences. This student is not on any medication for focus. Compare the normal brain in Scan 8 to the learning-different brain.

As you can see, Dr. Amen has been working hard to reveal the mysteries of the brain. His work over the last two decades has given answers not only to the medical community, but to parents and educators as well. He has clarified the unknown and given hope for thousands of people.

Behavior Problems

The AD/HD student is often an impulsive child, quick to react or strike out. He thinks of himself first and others later. This usually requires firm parents and cooperative teachers.

Terry is an adorable five-year-old who is the apple of his parents' eye. He greets everyone without hesitation and he knows everything there is to know about fish and fishing. He will try anything. Life to him is an adventure. These are the qualities of a leader.

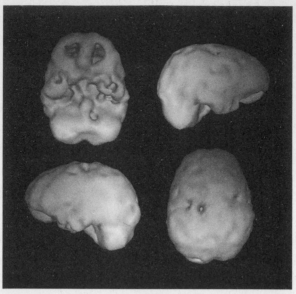

SCAN 7 (Courtesy of the Amen Clinic, Newport Beach, California)

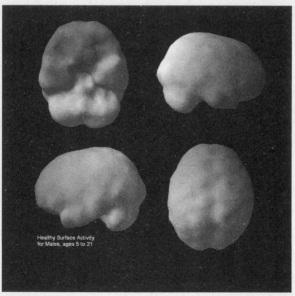

SCAN 8 (Courtesy of the Amen Clinic, Newport Beach, California)

In the classroom, Terry's feet are always on the back of the chair as he rocks back and forth. Sometimes he falls out of his chair. His teacher's response to him is to reprimand him and put his name on the board. It is hard for Terry to concentrate in the classroom because he concentrates on everything he sees. He observes every detail of the colorful bulletin board and analyzes the caterpillar on the windowsill, all while his teacher asks him for the answer to number 22.

Terry has been diagnosed with ADD, dyslexia and auditory processing disorder. Even though he has powerful strengths, his weaknesses, left unattended over time, will dampen his potential. In other words, a cute five-year-old who is impulsive can become an arrogant 11-year-old and an obnoxious 21-year-old. These wonderful ADD traits can benefit or hinder depending on how parents handle the diagnosis. Terry's parents have a long road ahead of them. They need to model proper social skills, because people like Terry have a hard time understanding how to gather inferences from others' body language (this will be discussed in later chapters).

When the parents of John, another of my students, received the diagnosis of AD/HD, they weren't quite sure how to go about disciplining him. Both parents thought that the other one was taking care of the discipline. In reality, he was getting away with murder at home and at school. I suggested to his mom and dad that they get some help with their parenting skills, because parenting an AD/HD child is not the same as parenting a child without it. I strongly recommend taking advantage of parenting programs for families with AD/HD children, such as the one at Southwestern Medical Center in the

Dallas area or at Children's Hospital in Orange County, California. Both facilities have helped countless families bring order and peace back into their homes.

AD/HD is not an excuse for bad behavior and it should never be used as one. It may be an explanation for certain behavior, but it cannot excuse it. If you tell a traffic cop who stops you for speeding that you have AD/HD, he will still give you the speeding ticket. If you tell the IRS you have AD/HD, you will still have to pay your taxes. If you tell your boss you have AD/HD, you will still be expected to do your work. If you tell your wife you have AD/HD, she will still expect you to pay attention to her. The demands of everyday life do not yield to the diagnosis of AD/HD. It is up to the individual with AD/HD to adjust to the demands of everyday life.

> AD/HD is not an excuse for bad behavior and it should never be used as one.

You can and should use your knowledge of AD/HD to make your child's life go more smoothly. A person with AD/HD can avoid getting the speeding ticket by acknowledging her taste for high speed and deliberately driving more slowly. He can stave off the IRS by acknowledging his tendency to procrastinate and hiring a tax person to prepare his taxes every year. She can talk to her boss and work out a plan to adapt better to her workplace. He can come to an understanding with his wife, asking her to use hand signals or verbal cues to bring him back when he tunes out or involuntarily ceases paying attention.

It is very important for parents not to allow their children to use their learning difference as an excuse. But to do this successfully, parents must educate themselves fully about their child's learning difference and address their own learning differences. If you or your spouse is learning-different, it is very important to get an accurate diagnosis. It is important to face it so that we, as parents, can address the same issues in our children's lives. Adult remediation can come in the form of AD/HD coaching, medication, psychotherapy and a host of other possibilities. Dealing with everyone's learning differences properly and in a timely manner will make for a peaceful home.[5]

Medication for Hyperactivity

Your child was born with the "Edison gene" described in the introduction. These genes dictate either high or low levels of one or all of the brain chemicals called dopamine, norepinephrine and serotonin. Medication helps many children by leveling out chemical inconsistencies. Sometimes I hear parents say, "They will outgrow this" or "They just need to control themselves and then everything will be okay." But no one can outgrow a neurological misfire within their brain.

When a child has AD/HD, her brain is actually going to sleep while her body knows that it must stay awake to complete the task at hand. The constant movement is her body's effort to keep her brain awake. Her chemical levels are out of balance, which causes her body to go into a state of commotion. If her parents choose to ignore these behaviors in their child, her future will be clouded with frustration academically and socially. This frustration can lead to anger that can be transferred into the classroom, home life and an adulthood marred by failure.

Hyperactivity varies from person to person. Some people

report less hyperactivity at the onset of puberty, while others describe symptoms of impulsivity and a lack of inhibition control well into their adult years. In adolescence and adulthood, hyperactivity can take the form of agitation or irritability. These individuals must be taught organizational and time management skills at a young age to find success in their adult years. If the learning difference with hyperactivity is not treated early in life, many individuals find themselves dealing with depression.

Medication to control hyperactivity can be effective in some cases. If you choose to use medication, find a child neurologist or psychiatrist who specializes in learning differences to diagnose and treat your child. These physicians are more qualified and have a greater understanding of the most current treatments than do traditional pediatricians. A good rule of thumb is to try a trial of medication (approximately a month) to see if it

> If you choose to try medication, remember that it should be prescribed by a physician and administered under his or her supervision.

is a good fit for your child. Remember, medication is only a tool; it is not a cure (though it is sometimes a necessary tool for children to be successful).

Many parents are afraid that medication will somehow change their child into some kind of monster or that it will wreak havoc on their bodies. Or they think that their child might become addicted, which will set them on the road to becoming an addict of other substances. All of the above is not true. Medications that treat hyperactivity are no more dangerous than any other medicines approved for child use by the FDA. There is about 50-years' worth of research in this field now, and to date, these medications have not proved to be habit-forming. Studies have also demonstrated that they do not have long-term effect on growth when monitored by a doctor that specializes in working with this population.[6] But also know that medication is not for everyone. Some individuals' bodies cannot tolerate them. When that is the case, more structure at home and school, along with behavior therapy and the right parenting skills, can be the prescription for success. If you choose to try medication, remember that it should be prescribed by a physician and administered under his or her supervision. Parents should be in constant communication with the physician when the medications are being started because it is important to report any side effects.

David was in kindergarten. His IQ was 140, but he had difficulty with his letter sounds as well as identifying his letters. He could not write his name. He could not sit still for more than three minutes at a time. Due to the fact that he was so bright, he could understand that he was not able to keep up with his peers. He knew that something was wrong. So he began to act out in the classroom. He blurted out answers before he was supposed to and his peers did not include him in games.

I worked with David from kindergarten through the second grade. I was able to help him decode words, but through every session David could not sit still. He had to take a piece of paper and roll it up like a tube, and then look through the tube to see each word. Every time he made a mistake, he began to cry. His frustration level was out of control. I asked David if it was hard to make his body stop moving. David looked at me and said with a sigh, "I want to stop, but my body won't let me." Silent tears streamed down his face. His parents decided to try a trial of medication to see if it would help. After one week on medication, he was calm and focused and feeling good about his progress. For David, medication was the right tool.

Helping Your AD/HD Child Shine

Learning differences occur in varying combinations and severities that affect the length of time a child benefits from remediation and/or a specialized school. Most children with learning differences are in academic remediation for an average of two to three years, but if your child is dealing with AD/HD, then treatment for parenting skills and behavior modification may take longer.

There is no "cure" for AD/HD in the medical sense of the word, and that's why appropriate training and remediation are so important. Specific instruction is necessary for a student to overcome his or her deficits. With hard work on his or her part and consistent support from parents, the child can become effective in reading, writing, spelling and/or math and so overcome major difficulties.

Please be careful when anyone says that they can cure AD/HD, dyslexia or related disorders. I have heard that biofeedback is the magic cure. I have heard that if you exercise a certain way every day, you'll be cured. I have heard that my child will outgrow the disorder. There are people out there who try to take advantage of parents' emotions, but remember that learning differences are a neurological problem, not a motivational one. As parents, we want a quick fix and we'll do anything to find it. After all, we are used to getting what we want when we want it. Unfortunately, learning differences do not have a quick fix, and as such they can teach us a lesson in consistency and tenacity. And to be all he or she can be, your child needs every ounce of both from you.

The AD/HD child, like the dyslexic, usually has a normal or better-than-normal IQ and can achieve his or her intellectual potential if properly taught. There are many individuals who have led eventful and powerful lives, some of whom have been mentioned in earlier pages. The entertainment field is filled with AD/HD individuals, and many others have made great inroads in a variety of professional fields. This is important to know, because many children with AD/HD struggle with low self-esteem and need all the encouragement they can get.

The paradox is that many of them have a difficult time accepting praise and encouragement. They need and want reassurance, yet they have great difficulty believing it. Part of the reason is that criticism is more stimulating to the brain than praise. In general, most people remember a critical comment for years but forget yesterday's compliment. Additionally, the AD/HD individual has often built such a wall of negativity around himself that it is almost impossible for positive remarks to find their way to his core. They strike his outer wall and glance off like rubber-tipped arrows, barely even noticed by his inner being. Criticism, however, pierces the wall and finds its way right to the center of the self, where it joins all the other arrows sticking there. Worst of all is that critical arrows are often shot by the individual himself.

In its extreme form this may be obsessive-compulsive disorder, which is sometimes seen with AD/HD. But more often it is simply a drift of mind most people with AD/HD have, which is counter to the upbeat message they usually give out. They often feel more comfortable in paralytic states of self-criticism than in peaceful self-love.

How to put a sharp point on praise and blunt the criticism? This is one of the most important tasks when treating AD/HD people: to help them open their hearts and minds to feeling good about themselves. Psychotherapy can help. Coaching can help. Reassurance can help. Prayer can help. Physical exercise can help. Above all, I think the best antidote to the negativity that can permeate the AD/HD mind is love. This may be love of a person, of family, of a job, of a place or of a mission in life. Whatever it is, help your child find it. Help them find groups where they are appreciated. Teach them how important it is to love someone who loves them for who they are, not someone who corrects or criticizes them for who they are not.[7]

> The best antidote to the negativity that can permeate the AD/HD mind is love.

WHAT IS DYSLEXIA?

Dyslexia is a specific type of language difference caused by visual and auditory processing dysfunctions in a person with average or above-average intellectual ability. This dysfunction impairs the processes of reading, written expression and spelling.

When dyslexia, at the time called "aphasia," was first described in the late-1800s, some physicians believed it was caused by some kind of brain or cerebral vascular injury. A German physician named Adolph Kussmaul didn't buy the injury explanation, however, and he coined the phrase "word blindness" in 1877. Ten years later, Dr. Rudolph Berlin, an ophthalmologist, combined the Greek words *dys-* ("ill" or "difficult") and *lexis* ("word") to make a new word, *dyslexia*. As the years rolled on, various doctors tried a myriad of tests and educational practices to identify and treat those with dyslexia, but none seemed to help.

Then, in 1925, an American neurologist named Dr. Samuel T. Orton proposed the first theory of a specific learning difficulty. He believed that this population could learn to read if they could use their non-visual senses—touch, taste, smell and hearing. Then Anne Gillingham came on the scene in 1936, and she analyzed the structure of language and combined it with what Dr. Orton had discovered. Out of this research, she published *The Gillingham Manual*, which gave various teaching strategies for the dyslexic population. This teaching method is known today as the Orton-Gillingham method. Out of their work, various reading programs have been developed that have proven to be extremely effective for learning-different students.[8]

Many dyslexics are quite verbal and do excellent oral work in school, but their written work is slow and often looks like that of a younger child. The dyslexic processes written symbols more slowly than a normal reader and he is often slow to finish his work. His motor skills are usually average with weaknesses noted in rhythmic exercises. Math is usually his best subject. If he has any problems in math, it is usually seen in immediate recall of numbers and facts, in spatial errors or in a loss of the pattern of the math function he is doing.

Jack was a pure dyslexic, which is very rare. Traditionally, if a child is diagnosed with dyslexia, he shares other differences as well. For example, he may have difficulty with handwriting or math skills (this is called dyscalculia) or difficulty with attention (AD/HD). Jack was in the first grade and a great kid, always asking questions about the planets. He wanted to know everything he could about the Milky Way. He was an *A* student in math and he had a lot of friends. The only problem was that Jack could not spell. He could read on grade level, but his fluency was very stilted. When we began the SEE (Sequential English Education) Therapy, he could only spell phonetically. I taught him how to decode the words, and over time his fluency and decoding skills improved dramatically.

If your child has dyslexia, she will likely have difficulty with reading, writing and spontaneous spelling. English will usually be her most difficult subject. If she remains in a regular class without outside help, she may be characterized as lazy, a child who does not try as hard as she could. With tutoring or a special class, however, she can be helped to perform up to her mental potential. She may always have to work harder for good grades than the student without dyslexia, but with help she can succeed academically. Adult dyslexics have achieved in every profession through hard work and remediation because they can see what they are going to do perfectly before they execute the actual task. An Edison-gene child can achieve anything.

When the Cooper family first got the diagnosis of dyslexia for their son, Blair, they really didn't know what it all entailed.

They thought he was reading his words backward. Boy, were they wrong. They learned instead that as Blair looked at a word, he perceived it as a partial word or substituted one word for another. He might see the word "elephant" and say the word "eggplant." When he read a complete sentence, he traded out the word "the" for "it" or "but" for "at." This may not sound like such a big deal, but think about it: The slightest alteration in words can create a very different meaning. "The elephant ran around it and looked at the lion" is quite different from "The eggplant ran around the and looked but the lion." How do you think Blair did on his comprehension questions? He was great at compensating for his weakness by distracting the teacher and being the class clown. But his parents knew that they had to get help. Blair was diagnosed with dyslexia and auditory processing disorder and received remediation through the SEE Therapy for two-and-a-half years. He is now reading two levels ahead of his current grade and is achieving in all areas of his life.

I, too, share the world of dyslexia. You are probably wondering how in the world I was able to write a book. Let me tell you, it wasn't easy! (Thank God for spell-check!) The first time I was aware that I had dyslexia was after I graduated from college. My boss at the time noticed the errors I made on letters I typed for the company. I don't think a day passed when I didn't have some spelling errors—and this was in the days when the world had typewriters and correction fluid. You can imagine my frustration.

As a young student, I always found it laborious to read anything; I only read if I had to. When I was in first grade, I remember my teacher telling my mother, "She is so bright, but she is not working up to her potential." As a child, I had no idea what that meant. All I remember is feeling that I was always missing something. I was always trying to keep up with my peers, but didn't know why it was so difficult.

I was put into the "dummy" reading group during middle school. I knew that I didn't want to stay there, but there seemed to be no way out. At that time, no one understood what dyslexia was or why remediation was necessary, so I stumbled on through school, determined to work harder and achieve the best I knew how. As I look back now, I recognize how these difficulties shaped me into who I have become. I did not feel sorry for myself or angry at the world; I just became more determined with every failure that came my way.

My failures came in the form of teachers telling me that they expected more out of me. They always raised the bar and I always fell short. Others who experienced similar situations, however, heard these same words and became bitter and angry. Many of them never went on to college. Most stayed in the community where I grew up and learned a trade.

I am currently writing another book for learning-different adults about how to be successful within the workplace. While interviewing many prominent and successful individuals, I discovered a common theme: survival of the fittest. Those dyslexics who were raised within the last 20 to 30 years have learned to cope with their environment. Many have evolved into accomplished men and women, while many others have been destroyed by the wounds that the world has thrust upon them.

Today is a much better time to be dyslexic. The breakthroughs that have been made in neurology and genetics have been literally life-changing for many in this population. I predict that within the next 20 to 30 years, we will see a world where learning differences are understood at birth and remediation can take place at a very early age. We know now that the genetic code for dyslexia is set in place during the fifth to sixth month of gestation. If we can find ways to help infants who have been identified with dyslexia, this will allow children to enter school on a level playing field with their peers. The future looks bright!

> I predict that within the next 20 to 30 years, we will see a world where learning differences are understood at birth and remediation can take place at a very early age.

WHAT ARE THE RELATED DISORDERS?

Central Auditory Processing Disorder

Central Auditory Processing Disorder is a condition in which there is an inability to differentiate, recognize or understand sounds while both the hearing and the intelligence are normal. It is possible to remediate this difficulty through auditory drills; I have seen success with nearly all my students. I believe that the program in which I am trained (Sequential English Education, or SEE) has the best approach to retraining the ear's perception of the spoken word.

Dyscalculia

This is a learning difference that usually occurs with ADD or AD/HD but can occur by itself. It is a deficit in math. Remedial time depends on the severity of the problems and the student's age when remediation begins.

Dysgraphia

This motor function or visual spatial problem usually occurs along with the other learning differences. The student has great difficulty with handwriting. The grip of a dysgraphic child is like that of a much younger child. His or her handwriting is usually illegible, but an occupational therapist will have great success remediating this difficulty. (My own children share this trait. Both Jackie and Alicia hold their pencils with a death grip; I don't know how in the world they can produce any letters at all. I think that they hold their pencils that way just to see me go crazy. They always say, "Hey, Mom . . . look!" and there they are with their two front fingers wrapped around the pencil, scribbling away. Ugh! Will they ever learn?)

Written Language Disorder

Some students, usually those in kindergarten or first grade who show some struggle with learning to read, have processing difficulties. On a battery of diagnostics tests, they register at a significant delay level only in written expression (writing sentences, paragraphs, compositions). Many of these students have a difficult time producing a visual image of what they want to write down. Others don't know how or where to begin the task of writing. There are those who have both challenges. Usually this disorder responds to remediation in three to four years.

Dysphasia/Aphasia (Oral Language Disorder)

Students who have oral language disorder cannot make normal associations between words (labels) and people, objects or ideas. They have trouble comprehending what people say to them and difficulty expressing their own thoughts. This disorder usually is found in combination with other learning differences, making it a complex learning disability. Students with this difficulty usually have the best success with speech therapy to master the language around them.

* * *

Here are some spontaneous written examples from two children with some of the learning differences mentioned above.

> In spring im going to canda.
> In cada they speke French and Enlesh.
> In going to wst canda ner the mountens.
> In a small cowboy town nere the slop.
> Im going to kea there.

> My cat lead is a bug busy cat. He eats a lote. He is a cumse anmal. He gets in to fites. My uthr cat is tamy. She is black, bron and wit. her bred is cimese. She is a mene cat. The uthr one is nice.

As you can imagine, learning differences can hold kids back from becoming who God intended them to be. But as parents, it is our job to educate ourselves and guide our children through this maze of learning differences to becoming successful adults. In upcoming chapters, we look at specific ways to do just that.

God's Purposes in Learning Differences

Every undertaking begins in discussion, and consultation precedes
every action. Here you can trace the mind's variety. Four kinds of
destiny are offered to men, good and evil, life and death; and always
it is the tongue that decides the issue. . . . If a man is wise and
instructs his people, then his good sense can be trusted. A wise man
will have praise heaped on him, and all who see him will count
him happy. The days of a man's life can be numbered,
but the days of Israel are countless.

ECCLESIASTICUS 37:16-18; 23-25[1]

Many people have a clouded and incomplete view of ADD, AD/HD, dyslexia and related disorders. Many still believe that the cause of these challenges is rooted in bad parenting, whether it's giving our children the wrong kind of food or not giving them the right kind of discipline. If you are the loving, conscientious parent of a child with learning differences, then you know first hand that this is just not the case.

Even with all the wonderful scientific strides made toward understanding learning differences, particularly during the past 50 years, most parents feel confused and lost when they first hear that their child has a learning difference. And while there are many theories out there that tell us what to do (more about these coming up), none of them tell us how God desires us to proceed.

If we look through Scripture, we find several people who share some of the characteristics of our learning-different population today. Take Moses, for example, who had a severe speech impediment. Pointing to his poor articulation skills, Moses begged God to choose someone else to speak to Pharaoh about freeing God's people from slavery in Egypt (see Exod. 4:10-17). God told him, in essence, "Who do you think made you that way? Don't you see I have a plan?" God didn't leave Moses on his own, however; He sent Moses' brother, Aaron, to help him complete his mission . . . speech impairment and all.

Then there's John the Baptist. Think about it: He was "the voice crying aloud in the wilderness" (Luke 3:4) who said anything that came into his mind through the Holy Spirit. He wore only a loincloth and lived on a diet of locusts and honey. As a professional, I certainly see poor social skills and impulsivity. I wonder what his parents, Elizabeth and Zechariah, thought and felt . . . perhaps they blamed themselves for John's "crazy" behavior and wondered if the people of Judea would accept his message more readily if he wasn't so "out there." If you're the parent of an impulsive, high-energy child, you have probably had similar thoughts and feelings. Parents

> It seems obvious from God's Word that He has no problem working with people who are different . . . in fact, He seems to prefer it!

want their children to be valued within their society, whether it is first-century Palestine or twenty-first-century North America.

Moses and John the Baptist are just two of the many people God has used for His purposes whose abilities, behavior or thought processes run against the grain of what is considered "normal." It seems obvious from God's Word that He has no problem working with people who are different . . . in fact, He seems to prefer it!

God never makes a mistake. When there is a challenge in our lives or in our children's lives, it means that God is giving us an opportunity to stretch and grow to our fullest potential. Many times, what looks to us like a real problem turns out to be a tremendous blessing.

God calls us to really look at, to reflect on, the situations He allows in our lives. The noise of the world is a constant distraction, and often we add to the world's noise with our mouth constantly moving and our thoughts and feelings whirling. But how can we hear what His plan is for us if we do not take the time to quiet ourselves and listen?

God also calls us to search for wisdom through His guidance. Your child has wonderful gifts and talents that can only be revealed in God's timing as He reveals His perfect plan. How will you choose to see your child? Will you see him or her as a good gift from God, or as someone who will drag you and everyone around them down throughout their lives? It's all in how you see them. Your perceptions and attitudes will set the tone for your child to succeed or fail. These are tough words, but they are words that must be heard and accepted if real growth is to occur. Let me introduce you to two families who have gone down very different paths according to their perceptions and attitudes.

I met a family early on in my practice that did not receive their child's diagnosis of auditory processing disorder, dyslexia, ADD and dysgraphia until he was a young adult. Because they did not seek the help he needed when he was young, they felt that they had failed their son miserably. Besides not seeking remediation that would have helped him thrive, they couldn't help but reflect on how their attitudes had affected him as he was growing up, negative attitudes they had done nothing to hide from him.

From the time he was a young boy, the son perceived himself to be stupid and unworthy to have any kind of happiness in his life. His father was embarrassed by his lack of success; the boy was uncoordinated and sports were difficult for him. The father put him in sports anyway, believing that he could coach his son into success. This just added to the boy's frustration. On top of that, the parents ignored his academic difficulty, saying things like, "Learn to deal with it. It can't be that hard." The son eventually dropped out of high school during his sophomore year. He began to self-medicate and was in and out of rehab for several years.

We met just after he had gotten out of rehab. The young man was trying to get his life on track again. Through hours of remediation therapy and life-skill development, he was able to turn the corner and find meaning and joy in his life. After all the pain and heartache, begun in a family with damaging attitudes, his turnaround was one of God's miracles. By all accounts, he should have been one of the statistics.

On the other hand, I know many families who have created warm and nurturing surroundings for their learning-different children. The Anderson family, for example, discovered that all three of their children, two boys and a girl, had learning differences in varying degrees. The boys were twins, and both suffered with speech delays. Jason, the older twin by three minutes, was diagnosed as dyslexic and had auditory processing difficulties, while Jacob, the younger, was diagnosed with AD/HD.

By the time they entered second grade, they were receiving therapy for their difficulties. Their sister, Julie, was diagnosed with auditory processing disorder before she entered third grade. The Andersons sought out the right therapists to remediate their children as early as possible, and kept them in therapy as long as was needed (four to six years for each child). That kind of time and financial commitment made it possible for their children to thrive in school and in life. Because they are being raised in a family that values their differences and gives them the tools they need to achieve, the Anderson kids can anticipate bright futures.

On the following page is a chart to help you evaluate your words and actions toward your child. Ask yourself what kind of impact you're making. Is your behavior positive or negative? Try to answer each question honestly. You can only become stronger when you know where your weaknesses lie.

Many parents feel guilty if they answer "yes" on some or most of the questions in columns one and three, but please remember: Even if you have not done as well as you would like in the past, you can change your perspective on and attitude toward your child for the future. With God's grace, you can begin

Behaviors	Random Acts of Kindness	Regrets (Verbal / Physical)
Do I yell when my child does not respond to requests?	Do I tell my child at least two positive things a day?	Have I said hurtful things to my child about his/her learning difference?
Do I think that with more discipline, my AD/HD child will be more attentive?	Do I show my child the positive things about his/her learning difference?	Have I ever been physically abusive toward my child because of his/her learning difference?
Do I speak for my child when he/she is in a group?	Have I enrolled my child in an athletic program where he/she can compete against him/herself?	Have I ever told my learning-different child that he/she is lazy?
Do I share my child's difficulties with my peers, especially when my child is present?	Do I teach my child how to help others in his/her community?	Have I shown my child that I am disappointed in him/her because of his/her learning difference?
Do I excuse my child's bad behavior because of his/her learning difference?	Do I show my child the necessary social skills to be successful?	Have I avoided spending time with my child?
	Do I show my child that I love him/her no matter what?	Have I ever wanted someone else to deal with my child's learning difference?

to see and treat your child as the wonderful, God-made creation that he or she is. The next two exercises will help you do just that.

Write a letter to your child, a letter for your eyes only; it's not meant to be delivered. Write down all the mistakes that you have made and ask for your child's forgiveness. At the end of the letter, tell your child how you intend to change for the better. Be as specific as possible. Make it in list form if you need to. Writing down your thoughts and intentions will help you clarify your goals and next steps. When you've done that, you're ready to look more objectively at your child and his or her learning difference.

> With God's grace, you can begin to see and treat your child as the wonderful, God-made creation that he or she is.

In each column of the table on the following page, circle the characteristics that most accurately describe your child. Then, using the characteristics you have circled as a reference, describe your child in sentence form. Here is an example: "My child is calm, but fidgets with anything that is put in front of him. He has fair self-esteem and average intelligence." As parents, we tend to exaggerate what we perceive as our children's weaknesses, and this is a great tool to help you see your child more objectively. When you do so, you are seeing your child through God's eyes and can more easily recognize what he or she brings to the world.

I firmly believe that whether or not your child has a learning difference, God has a plan to use him or her mightily for

Symptoms	Daily Issues	Family Factors
Calm/fidgets	Self-esteem: good/fair	Difficulty falling asleep: Yes / No
Easy going/ aggressive	Intelligence: Low / Average / High	Difficulty waking up: Yes / No
High energy/ lethargic	Gets along with friends: Yes / No	Restless: Yes / No
Happy/depressed	Inattentive: Yes / No	Self-centered: Yes / No
Pleasant/irritable		
Charming/sullen	Impulsive: Yes / No	Accident prone: Yes / No
Class clown/shy		
Relaxed/anxious	Disorganized: Yes / No	Interrupts/butts in: Yes / No
Cautious/daring		
Tenacious/gives up easily	Loses things: Yes / No	Two-parent family: Yes / No
Compliant/defiant	Forgets things: Yes / No	Step-parents: Yes / No
Copes well/easily frustrated	Complies with requests: Yes / No	Family understands AD/HD (supportive): Yes / No
Angry outbursts/ calm	Will do chores: Yes / /No	Reasonable discipline: Yes / No
Talks a lot/quiet and low-key	Truthful: Yes / No	Open communication: Yes / No
	Responds to medication: Yes / No	Relatives understand AD/HD (supportive): Yes / No
		Family stresses (money, illness, divorce, remarriage): Yes / No
		Attending the same school: Yes / No

His glory. Yes, coping with learning differences is difficult at times for both parents and children, but if we truly believe that God is sovereign and that His Word is trustworthy, we can be assured that He is working all our circumstances (even learning differences!) together for His glory (see Rom. 8:28). If that is true, then we can see our children as He sees them: fashioned in His image to reflect His glory as He works His will in their lives.

SECTION TWO

PARENTING YOUR LEARNING-DIFFERENT CHILD

3

What's a Parent to Do?

And he will turn away from listening to the truth and wander into myths.

2 TIMOTHY 4:4

I recently received an article from a friend, who had clipped it from the "Dear Abby" column of her local newspaper.

> I am often asked to describe the experience of raising a child with a disability to try to help people who have not shared that unique experience to understand it, to imagine how it would feel. It's like this. . . .
>
> When you're going to have a baby, it's like planning a fabulous vacation trip to Italy. You buy a bunch of guidebooks and make your wonderful plans. You can't wait to see the Coliseum, Michelangelo's *David*, the gondolas in Venice. You may learn some handy phrases in Italian. It's all very exciting.
>
> After months of eager anticipation, the day finally arrives. You pack your bags and off you go. Several hours later the plane lands. The stewardess comes in and says, "Welcome to Holland."
>
> "Holland?!?" you say. "What do you mean, Holland? I signed up for Italy! I'm supposed to be in Italy. All my

life I've dreamed of going to Italy."

"But there's been a change in the flight plan. They've landed in Holland and there you must stay."

The important thing is that they haven't taken you to a horrible, disgusting, filthy place, full of pestilence, famine and disease. It's just a different place.

So you must go out and buy new guidebooks. And you must learn a whole new language. And you will meet a whole new group of people you would never have met.

It's just a different place. It's slower-paced than Italy, less flashy than Italy. But after you've been there for a while and you catch your breath, you look around, and you begin to notice that Holland has windmills, Holland has tulips, Holland even has Rembrandts.

But everyone you know is busy coming and going from Italy, and they're all bragging about what a wonderful time they had there. And for the rest of your life, you will say, "Yes, that's where I was supposed to go. That's what I had planned."

But if you spend your life mourning the fact that you didn't get to Italy, you may never be free to enjoy the very special, the very lovely things about Holland.[1]

As a parent navigates through the murky waters of the unknown (whether in Italy or Holland, Illinois or Alabama), they must avoid drowning in the Sea of Denial. I have met so many parents who have chosen this path for their families. When a parent is in denial, the child can lose remediation time, fall further behind in school and even begin to find unhealthy ways of dealing with his or her differences. If parents can maneuver these waters successfully, on the other hand, then their child will be on track to share his or her gifts with the world. Who knows? He or she could be the next Einstein.

There are six currents in the Sea of Denial, and we will take a closer look at each one in this chapter. There are also five responses common among parents who find out their child is learning-different. Only one of these will help them cross the Sea of Denial to the other side.

The good news is that there are also lifeboats that can help anyone who needs them to maneuver through each current. These lifeboats include prayer, language and speech therapists, learning-different schools and family support, and we'll explore each of these as well, in upcoming chapters.

First, let's look at the currents that make the Sea of Denial so dangerous.

CURRENTS IN THE SEA OF DENIAL

Not My Child!

The "Not my child!" current is often the initial, knee-jerk parental reaction to a child's diagnosis. Parents feel that there has been some mistake. They say to themselves, *My child is so bright! There's no way he has AD/HD*. As parents swirl in circles through this current, some choose to get a second opinion, which is fine as long as doing so is not a delay tactic. At worst, they ignore the diagnosis and drop the matter altogether.

I met Cory when he was 19. He had been out of substance-abuse rehab for one year and was trying to get back on his feet. He had been recently diagnosed with dyslexia and AD/HD and didn't really know what that meant, but he knew that he had to figure it out if he was going to make it.

When Cory was a child, he had difficulty in school with reading and was always in trouble for something. His parents knew that he had dyslexia, but they thought that this "dyslexia thing" was something that the public schools just made up when they couldn't figure out what to do with a kid. They refused the suggested treatment that the school offered; they believed that Cory would be fine if they just ignored the whole thing. Obviously, this was not the case.

Now it was up to Cory not to ignore his diagnosis. He had to step up to the plate and help himself. I worked with Cory for about six months. He started back to college and had his eye on becoming a paramedic. The game plan that Cory created for himself was very doable, but unfortunately, he stopped coming to his sessions. His impulsivity caused him to make the wrong choices and he is now serving time for drug possession.

Is there hope for Cory? Yes! Cory is a child of God. God did not make a mistake with him. But Cory's parents should have given him the proper groundwork he needed as a child by accepting his diagnosis and getting the help he needed. Instead, they were swept into the "Not my child!" current in the Sea of Denial and ignored the problem. Today, if Cory sticks to the therapies (psychotherapy, language therapy, as well as spiritual support), there is every chance he will turn his life around. Will it take time? Will it be difficult? You bet. But Cory is worth it.

In the Fog

I can't tell you how many parents live in this current for years without coming out on the other side. The fog seeps in when parents suspect that their child may have a learning difference, but they have not gotten professional testing to confirm their suspicions. These parents may not have access to proper testing facilities or may not have funds available to get testing. They may have received preliminary testing in the public schools, but the results were not explained effectively to them. Due to a lack of guidance and direction, they live in a fog, only able to guess at what to do for their child. Once these parents are directed to the right testing facility and receive the proper diagnosis, however, the fog clears and they paddle directly through the Sea of Denial with no problem.

Janice was in the fog for 15 years. She had three children, two boys and a girl, all of whom had learning differences. I met Janice when I spoke at a homeschool conference in Kansas City. She and her husband believed that homeschooling was the best thing for their children spiritually, but as their academic years unfolded, she realized that they had learning difficulties. Their family lived in a small town in Missouri and, to her knowledge, there was not a testing facility available. The Internet was her sole source of education on AD/HD, dyslexia and related disorders. She tried the latest reading programs, self-help books and any seminars she could attend to understand her children's challenges, but all the while, her children were not receiving the proper remediation to bring them up to their reading potential.

At the conference in Kansas City, I recommended Janice take her children to be tested at the Shelton Evaluation Center in Dallas, Texas. I knew that it would be a bit of a drive, but I was confident that the effort would be worth it when Janice's kids received the help they needed. Janice followed through with my suggestion and was directed to a language therapist in her area. Today, her children are succeeding in their high school and college curricula.

Get Help and Move On

Once some parents have realized that there may be a problem, they may be open to getting some help for their child, but under the surface, they want to get it over with as soon as possible. Whatever therapy is suggested, they will do, and they tend to be proud of themselves for getting on top of things quickly . . . even as they minimize their child's difficulty with family and friends. It's important for them to give the outward appearance that this is a minor problem, a hiccup in the educational career of their child. That may be the case for certain children, but for many others, learning differences will be a lifelong issue. Parents must come to terms with the fact that learning differences are a misfire in the brain, a misfire their child will deal with all his or her life. There is no cure for learning differences. Remediation therapies can rewire neural pathways for learning to be more effective, but their child may have social and educational difficulties with varying severity throughout their lives.

When parents get stuck in this current, they do a disservice to their child. Even if their child begins to see success after remediation in the primary school years, he or she may have difficulty again in junior high or high school. At that time, phase two of therapy may be needed. This makes perfect sense when you consider that when a greater quantity of information is given, the brain must process more quickly. Many parents who just want to get help and move on, however, mistakenly believe that additional remediation is not necessary. They end up going around and around in the Sea of Denial until their child is failing again.

> Parents must come to terms with the fact that learning differences are a misfire in the brain, a misfire their child will deal with all his or her life.

Jacob's parents were devastated when they learned that their son was diagnosed with AD/HD and dyslexia. The learning specialist at Jacob's school referred them to me, and early on, they were committed to doing whatever possible to help their son. Jacob was always willing to work and he moved through the remediation process with ease, and after two-and-a-half years of hard work, he was ready to stay in the classroom setting without my help. His parents were thrilled that he was now reading two levels above his current grade. Everything seemed great.

Two years later, Jacob was having difficulty with his written expression. It took him hours to get his thoughts down on paper. Many times he became so frustrated that he cried, and family arguments ensued. Jacob's mother called and was very angry with me. She felt that his difficulties were my fault and that I should have taken care of everything when I worked with him two years before.

When a parent does not comprehend that a child's learning difference is with him for life, this is not an uncommon response. In the early stages of therapy, the focus is on rewiring the brain to master decoding and auditory skills. After this has been achieved, often dyslexic and AD/HD students later have difficulty with written expression. If and when this occurs, the second phase of therapy must begin to teach students how to articulate their spoken and written word. Not all dyslexic and AD/HD students experience this additional challenge, so it is important to take a break after initial therapy to see how the student responds in the traditional classroom.

To sum up, it is important for parents not to get stuck in this current. Your child may need various forms of therapy as you proceed through his or her academic career. Don't be afraid to get it when you need it, and move forward from there.

Are We There Yet?

All parents want to hear that the difficulty of their child's learning difference is finally over. They don't want to see their child suffer.

If we could, most of us would suffer in our child's place. But we can't. This is a road God intended for them, and we must guide them through the rough waters . . . even when they are tired of swimming.

Hannah was diagnosed with ADD, dyslexia and dysgraphia. She began therapy with me when she was in first grade, and her mom and dad were very excited to get to the bottom of her problems. I saw Hannah twice a week for 45 minutes each session. She had a very hard time focusing; she could only stay focused for about three minutes at a time. I used all the manipulatives (squishy ball, bumpy cushion, thera-band, etc.) available to help her stay on task.

Even with her challenges, Hannah made good gains through her first-grade year. When she entered second grade, however, she became bored with therapy. Hannah manipulated her parents into believing she was finished with the remediation program. Mom and Dad were tired of the commitment and wanted to be done as well, so they ended Hannah's therapy before true remediation could be achieved. Unfortunately, she regressed. Hannah is now back where she started a year and a half ago.

Remember, you are the parent. Stand tough. When your child begins to buck therapy, remediation is working. When the brain is being rewired, it's not easy. Think of someone who needs physical therapy for his or her broken leg: It hurts to move that leg, but if they don't, it will never work well again. They must do what it takes to make that leg work properly, even when doing so is pure misery.

Your child may try anything to get out of therapy, but if the process is interrupted, any rewiring of the brain may be lost. When therapy begins again, the student must begin from the beginning. You must stay committed or their future success will be compromised.

Self-Pity

Most parents generally go through a period of depression after finding out about their child's learning difference. This is natural; parents need to mourn the loss of the future they imagined in order to embrace the future that will be. It's okay to be sad for a little while that you ended up in Holland instead of Italy.

It is a good idea to make sure that your spouse paddles through this current with you; it is easier to get past this one together and avoid turning depression into self-pity. Self-pity drags everyone down, including your children.

Kathy knew cognitively that her daughter Abby's diagnosis of AD/HD was not her fault, but deep down inside, she wasn't so sure. She kept wondering if she could have done something different during her pregnancy or during Abby's early years to avoid the problem.

Kathy was a straight-*A* student and in the top of her class in high school. She received a full scholarship to the university of her choice. In Kathy's imagination, her children would find the same type of success. When she received Abby's diagnosis, however, all she could see was her struggling daughter barely holding it together. At parent-teacher conferences, she would hear, "Abby does not stay on task," "She doesn't turn in her homework on time," "She seems to be so day-dreamy in class," and "If she doesn't get it together soon, she will have to repeat the grade or find another school."

> Self-pity drags everyone down, including your children.

Kathy felt depressed as she grieved the loss of the future she imagined for her precious daughter. She eventually got help through her child's school counselor. Abby came to me for re-mediation. Kathy and I talked about having learning-different children, and I was able to convince her that it was largely her attitude and approach that would determine Abby's future. If she thought Abby would fail, then she probably would fail. And if she could show Abby her strengths and help her work on her weaknesses, then Abby could achieve her own success. Kathy began to understand, and she adapted to a new view of her daughter. Instead of wallowing in self-pity, Kathy helped Abby thrive and become who she was meant to be.

Pride

Most of us don't want to hear that we might be motivated by pride, the last of the dangerous currents in the Sea of Denial. After all, we have given our whole lives to our children and our spouses. That makes us loving and giving people, right? Well, guess what: Pride was the downfall of humanity (and that includes parents).

Many of us think that we can deal with learning-different problems ourselves. We don't need anyone. "My child will be fine. We're taking care of it. Everyone, just leave us alone." When you're stuck, swirling around, in this current, you feel anger toward people who try to help. If you're not careful, you may even feel bitterness toward your child. To guard against pride, you must realize that learning differences are not about you! This is your chance to give your child an opportunity to live a great life. This is your chance to get over yourself and move toward what God intends for both you and your child. Humbling yourself to ask God and others for help will smooth out the rough currents of pride.

Jena and Carl had five children, and three shared a plethora of learning differences. Jena and Carl had many learning-different traits as well, but they never had formal diagnoses. When their children were diagnosed, they didn't believe they had dyslexia or AD/HD; they simply had minor reading problems that needed attention. Jena and Carl told the school that they never wanted to hear the words "dyslexia" or "AD/HD" used with regard to their children. If the words were said by mistake, Jena would break into tears. The children did receive remediation for their learning differences through the school, but when Jena and Carl realized their kids were in therapy with other learning-different children, they were removed from the remediation they desperately needed.

Their pride was more important than their children's welfare. Jena and Carl were embarrassed and ashamed, and their decisions were based on how they would be perceived by their peers rather than on the wellbeing of their children.

Be honest with yourself: Are you embarrassed or ashamed that your child is learning-different? Make sure preserving your pride is not your central motivator. Your children deserve better from you.

FIVE RESPONSES TO THE DIAGNOSIS

There are five main responses parents choose when they find out their child is learning-different. Only one, the last, is helpful to them and their child over the long term.

1. Don't Ask, Don't Tell

Don't-ask-don't-tell parents respond to their child's diagnosis by saying, "I know my child has a problem. Of course I want to get him the help that he needs, but I don't want to broadcast it all over town. Nobody needs to know." They usually don't tell anyone about their child's struggles unless they know another parent with a learning-different child. Then they have a misery-loves-company attitude.

I saw Mrs. Cassini the other day at one of the schools where I work. I have seen her often and it is obvious how involved she is at the school. She is the head of the P.T.A. and is always available to help out in her children's classroom or on field trips. Her second-grade daughter, Cassy, was diagnosed with dyslexia, dysgraphia and auditory processing disorder. I know because I work with Cassy two days a week.

I overheard Mrs. Cassini talking with her peers at the school about Cassy. One of them asked, "Didn't Cassy have some trouble with reading this year?" Mrs. Cassini said, "Oh, no. She was just in the wrong reading group. Once the teacher figured out that she needed more of a challenge, she was fine." Then she looked over at me and waved. (Huh?)

The next day, I saw Mrs. Cassini talking to the parent of another child who sees me for remediation. The two of them were comparing notes on how much longer their children would be in therapy. They stood outside my therapy room for at least an hour before they came in to ask about their children.

This response makes a parent very susceptible to the currents of pride and self-pity in the Sea of Denial.

2. Beat Around the Bush

These parents are always trying to find someone to agree that there is nothing wrong with their child. They get the help their child needs, but the first time a teacher tells them that their child is doing well, they are quick to discontinue the remediation process. Obviously, this response leads directly into the "Are we there yet?" current in the Sea of Denial, because beat-around-the-bush parents are eager to listen to their learning-different child when they say, "Mom or Dad, I don't think I really need this therapy. It's not working for me."

I began working with Kevin early in his first-grade year. He had difficulty with auditory processing, attention and dyslexia. He could focus for only short periods of time. He knew only 10 letters of the alphabet by sight and could not recognize several of the letters' sounds. Obviously, reading was a struggle for him.

Kevin did very well in therapy for about one year. As we progressed into the most pivotal part of therapy, Kevin's parents saw his improvement and decided that his learning difference wasn't as severe as they had been told. When they found out that Kevin's second-grade teacher took a course on learning differences over the summer, they were anxious to believe that she could meet what they felt were his very minor needs. And when Kevin expressed his boredom with our remediation sessions, they were sucked into the dangerous current.

3. Play the Blame Game

Some parents respond by blaming everyone else for their pain and disappointment. They blame their spouse for the learning differences within their family. They blame administrators or therapists if their child is not remediated according to their timetable. The irony is that blaming others is a typical trait of those with ADD. Many times, it is the blame-game playing parent who has passed on the gene to their child.

The learning-different adult is often not aware of how selfish they can be. Their mindset is usually, "Me first, you later." Many times they feel that the world owes them something. This stems from the fact that they were likely undiagnosed as children and the world has been very unkind to them. As their families come along, they tend to have a fearless attitude toward the world because they have a tight family unit where they are finally accepted for who they are. Unfortunately, they were never taught proper social skills, so now they are flying by the seat of their pants. Many of these individuals have very few friends but many acquaintances because their intense personalities scare people away.

Clare was always on the go. She wanted her life to be filled with excitement and constant change; she loved the rush of adrenaline. As each of her children was born, she had another reason to fill her life with more activity. Routine and consistency were not in her vocabulary. She never had dinner on the table the same time; dinner was served when she could fit it into the schedule. It was not uncommon to have her children start their homework at 10:00 P.M. She had no idea that this constant motion was her own ADD in full swing.

Clare received a call from her son's teacher, who wanted to let her know that he was having trouble at school. She had some measures taken to help him succeed, and Clare said, "Sure, do whatever you need to do." The teacher gave Clare information about tutors, remediation therapists and speech therapists and expected her to follow through. But when conference time rolled around and Clare's son was failing miserably, Clare became indignant with the teacher. She didn't understand why the teacher had not taken care of her son. When the teacher asked Clare why she hadn't called the therapists on the list, Clare replied, "I pay my taxes for you to do those things. You really should do your job." Clare's son was the loser because she chose to play the blame game.

4. Do Nothing

Do-nothing parents believe that if they just let their child alone, he or she will grow out of their problems. But as we've seen, learning differences are neurological; brain wiring doesn't change without intentional effort.

Luke and Anna had a son who was "all boy." He was into everything and loved sports, at which he excelled. However, they began to see a pattern of bizarre behavior: Whenever he was in the classroom for any length of time, he became agitated and started fights with anyone who was close. He also had difficulty reading. Luke and Anna believed that their son's behavior was age appropriate and that he would simply outgrow his outbursts. After all, Luke could remember when he used to act the same way at his son's age. If Luke had turned out okay, surely his son would be just fine.

> When parents respond to their child's learning differences by not responding, the shore on the far side of the sea never gets any closer.

Doing nothing can all too easily lead to getting caught in the dangerous currents lurking in the Sea of Denial, if the parents ever cross at all. When parents respond to their child's learning differences by *not* responding, the shore on the far side of the sea never gets any closer.

5. Take One Day at a Time

When parents respond by taking one day at a time, they will navigate the Sea of Denial effectively. They work as a team and don't stay too long in any one current. They are not afraid to revisit therapy when their child needs it. They usually have a great attitude about their situation and don't take each other too seriously. These parents raise healthy adults who understand how to live and work with their learning differences.

Rita and Joe had a difficult time having children; trying consumed almost 14 years of their life together. Failed fertility procedures nearly broke them financially, and they were physically and emotionally drained. One day after church, where their story was common knowledge, a young woman approached them. She was about to deliver a baby girl, and knew that she was too young to keep her. She had just been offered a full scholarship to Julliard and knew that her baby needed a home more stable than she could give. She asked Rita and Joe if they would raise her daughter as their own. Julia was a gift that totally overwhelmed them, but when she was born, she immediately became the apple of her parents' eyes.

I met Julia when she was in first grade. She was a sweet child with big brown eyes and long, flowing brown hair. You might be inclined to think that Rita and Joe spoiled her, but that was definitely not the case. Julia was generous and kind, and was always there for her peers. Unfortunately, her peers were not as kind in return. Her learning difference caused her to miss many inferences in her social world. Kids teased her when she read poorly or did not understand how to play a game fast enough.

Rita and Joe knew that Julia needed remediation, and they never missed a lesson. When we neared the end of her first phase of therapy, they asked what they could expect in the future; they wanted to be prepared, if and when phase two was needed. When Julia completed her early remediation, she read on a sixth-grade level in third grade.

As Rita and Joe continue to take one day at a time, they ensure that Julia's future remains bright.

ON THE OTHER SIDE OF THE SEA

Once on the other side of the Sea of Denial, your family's life can be prosperous and filled with the joy of God's promise. He only wants good things for you, and His purpose for your child will become clear as he or she grows in Him. Perhaps you are raising a child that will bring intellectual greatness to our planet. Or maybe you are raising a child with a gentle spirit who will quietly spread the Kingdom through her deeds of kindness and love. On the other side of the Sea of Denial, you can look forward to seeing your child's future unfold with faith in the God who holds him or her in His hands.

When Amy and Steve Stillman realized that their two children, Peter and Casey, had learning differences, they were shocked. They knew Peter and Casey both had difficulty reading and paying attention in class, but dyslexia and AD/HD? That couldn't be! However, as the Stillman children progressed through school, their struggles became ever more obvious. Casey could not stay seated for more than four minutes at a time. She seemed to do well when asked to read out loud, but she could comprehend nothing. Peter was dyslexic and hated to read for any period of time. To break a word down took him several minutes.

Amy and Steve, typical parents of learning-different children, realized they needed help. The difference between the

Stillmans and other families mentioned here is that the Stillmans crossed the Sea of Denial and moved forward as a team to tackle their family's problems. They were consistent, making sure that neither Peter nor Casey missed a therapy session. They created a family atmosphere of joy and peace by talking and learning about their children's learning differences. In fact, both Amy and Steve were diagnosed with learning differences as they sought remediation for their kids. They have embraced who they are as a family and have crossed the Sea of Denial without getting caught in the currents.

Whatever your initial response to your child's diagnosis, remember to ask God to be the center of your family's life. He will guide you where your child will be most successful, and He will guide you as you make your crossing of the Sea of Denial. Be quiet and listen. He will give you the answers you are looking for. Life is full of twists and turns, and you have been chosen to share in your child's journey. So enjoy the ride and hang on tight!

4

Good News About Bad Behavior

BEHAVIOR

Every parent observes odd or inappropriate glitches in their child's behavior from time to time. This is normal. But when inappropriate behaviors are not outgrown or become a regular pattern, it is time to get some professional help to understand what the behaviors are telling you. When I speak at various conferences and parent workshops, parents want to know how to identify learning differences in their toddlers. Here is a good way to distinguish these behaviors.

The normal behavior of a toddler can often mimic the behavior of an AD/HD child. They can have an unusually high level of energy (always on the go) and their attention span is short. They often have temper tantrums when they don't get their way. It's not uncommon to hear parents of toddlers say, "Johnny is driving my crazy! He is so ADD today." That may or may not be the case. As your child transitions from the toddler years to preschool age, the C.L.A.P. acronym can help alert you to behaviors that may indicate a learning difference. In addition, an occupational therapist can help you identify any problems your child has with sensory integration.

Coordination
Language
Attention
Perception[1]

Coordination

Be on the lookout for how your child is doing in the areas of fine and gross motor skills. For fine motor skills, observe how well she uses scissors to cut paper. How well does she grip a pencil? Can she pour water from a small pitcher into a glass? Can she string beads together without difficulty? Mastering these skills influences future reading skills.

Between the ages of three and five, children are ready to hold a pencil or crayon properly. Don't just think it's cute if your child holds the pencil or crayon with a death grip; if he or she cannot master a proper hold by the time he or she is five, there may be a weakness in reading later on. Show him how to hold scissors correctly. Model for her how to cut and how to draw lines in circular motions.

For gross motor skills, observe how well your child kicks or catches a ball. How well does she run? Can he skip, jump rope or ride a bike? The large muscle groups in the body control all of these activities. Most toddlers struggle to learn these activities, but if your child still has difficulty as he or she is entering first grade, this may indicate reason for concern. (Parents who are floating in the Sea of Denial may think at this point, *This is ridiculous! I still hold my pen with a death grip, and I read just fine.* To these folks I put this question: *How was school for you? Did you sail through or did you have difficulty? Do you want your child to have a similar experience?*)

If you see red flags in both fine and gross motor skills, I encourage you to get your child evaluated; he or she may be at risk for learning differences.

Language

When our children learn to talk, it is the greatest thing in the world. They are beginning to recognize their world and in that world, *we* are the center. Never in our lives has someone thought so much of us!

Often when children begin to communicate, they use a language only parents can understand. This is normal. The problem comes when Mom or Dad has to interpret their child's language for the rest of the world as he or she gets older.

Imagine that your nephew, Johnny, is nearly three years old. At a family gathering, he expresses that he needs something from you. Johnny's words sound something like, "Aut, aut, ese," and you can't understand what he is asking . He becomes more and more agitated when he sees that he is not communicating well enough to get what he wants. Just then, his mother races to the scene and informs you that Johnny *wants water, please.* "Of course he does!" you say. (*Why didn't he say so?* you think.)

Try to avoid baby talk or your "secret talk" when your child begins to use words. It may sound like his own language coming from the tower of Babel (see Gen. 11:4-9). Use clear language that can be understood by the majority of people. As you do, keep tabs on your child's developing language and communication skills. If he or she persists in word mispronunciation or misuse, keep an eye out for other behavioral indicators. (Parents still in denial may think, *But Johnny is so cute when he talks like that! He'll grow out of it. No need to overreact to such a silly thing.* To them I say, *Baby talk is only cute when babies use it. Do you really want Johnny to feel isolated and frustrated when he cannot make himself understood?*)

Attention

Most toddlers have poor attention due to the fact that their brains are still trimming back the number of neurons needed to succeed in their world. Attention from infancy to the age of three is somewhat variable and subjective.

But if your child reaches preschool age and has extreme difficulty following through on simple tasks, there might be reason for concern. An example is asking your child to go to her room and get her shoes, socks and red jacket and then she does not return. Or she returns with only one of the items and appears very happy with herself for completing that part of the task. If this behavior happens more often than not, then this child may be at risk for learning differences in the auditory processing area.

Some parents would interpret this as defiance or some kind of hearing impairment. I used to call it "selective hearing" before I realized that my child was dealing with it on a daily basis. Once I was educated that auditory processing disorder was a neurological misfire in the brain (not my child refusing to do what I told her), it all began to make sense.

In therapy, I teach parents to break down tasks into single steps for their child. I show them how to come down to Mary's eye level, and then ask her to get her shoes from her room and bring them to the parent. Then they ask Mary to repeat what they just asked her to do. When they know she understands their instruction, she is free to go and complete the task. When that task is complete, they repeat the exercise for her socks, and then for her red jacket. This approach may take a little longer, but most parents find themselves keeping their temper and their child feeling good about herself over her small accomplishments.

Perception

This area is concerned with what your child perceives about the relationships in the world around him. Let's say that Johnny is coloring with a friend and his friend chooses a crayon that Johnny was about to pick. Johnny assumes that his friend took the crayon from him on purpose, and a power struggle over the crayon is suddenly in full swing. Johnny perceives aggression where none is present. (Parents in denial may think, *This is just normal kid behavior. What's the big deal?* To a certain point, this is true—most young children struggle to learn how to share. But if confrontations of this nature regularly escalate to severe temper tantrums or to physical aggression, there *is* reason for concern.)

> It takes time for every child to learn social cues, but slowness to catch on may indicate a learning difference.

It takes time for every child to learn social cues, but slowness to catch on may indicate a learning difference. The boys are choosing sides for their game of kick ball. Johnny is picked last due to his poor coordination, and there are whispers of disappointment from the team as he is picked. Johnny smiles and is thrilled, oblivious to the whispers. The boys begin their game. As they rotate through their turns they skip Johnny, but he does not perceive that anything is wrong. He is just happy to be with everyone.

Girls who have learning differences also have difficulty with social perceptions. Mary comes up to some girls on the playground and steps very close to a friend's face to ask if she can play with them. Her friend steps back, agitated, and says firmly, "No."

Mary continues, "Let's play jump rope! I have one that I brought from home. It will be fun!"

Her friend says, "You're weird," and runs off.

Mary stands there, confused, and then asks another friend to play. The other girl says, "I guess so," and rolls her eyes with a look of annoyance. Mary misses the cue, thrilled to join her new friend. She has no concept of body language and social space.

Kids have an uncanny way of knowing when something is not quite right with their peers, and they let a child know, in no uncertain terms, that there is something wrong with him or her. It can be painful for parents to watch their child excluded or teased, even as he or she remains contentedly unaware that anything is amiss. (Parents in denial may think that exclusion of this kind is just "kids being kids." If their child is unaware of being excluded, however, this is likely not the case.)

Parents can help by modeling various body language situations. This may be difficult for some parents who are dealing with a perceptive disorder in their own lives. (Remember, learning differences are hereditary.) If perception is difficult for you, seek out someone you trust to help both you and your child understand how to work well in social settings. A child psychologist who specializes in children with learning differences or a speech therapist who offers social skill training is the best choice.

Children may also experience perception problems in reading. They may perceive letters in an incorrect order or trade whole words for others. This occurs when there is a misfire in the occipital area of the brain. The child sees a word accurately, but when it is processed through the brain, it is perceived differently. As your child learns to read, stay alert to any difficulties in perception.

Sensory Integration

One other behavioral trait you should watch for is a problem with sensory integration. Sensory integration is the inability of the brain to correctly process information brought in by the senses.

Children with sensory integration disorder (SID) can be either hyposensitive or hypersensitive to outside stimuli. For example, children who are hyposensitive to touch constantly crash into things, seeking extra stimulation, while the hypersensitive child avoids being touched or touching things when at all possible. SID can also include children who have processing deficits in one or more areas, such as visual or auditory processing. When a child has a visual processing deficit, they have a hard time finding words for objects they see; or if asked to get an object, they look right at it and then say they can't find it. They are seeing, but their brains are not processing what they are seeing. When a child has an auditory possessing deficit, he or she hears what is said, but the brain does not process it. The child may completely misunderstand or may take several minutes to understand before the information "clicks."

One way to help with auditory processing deficits is to break down directions, giving your child one thing to do at a time; let him finish the first task before you give him another instruction. Listening or music therapy can also help with auditory processing deficits.

Below is a list of other behaviors exhibited by children with SID:

- Loves to spin, swing and jump—doing so seems to calm them down after several minutes
- Complains of how clothing feels, does not like tags left in their clothing, has to have their socks on just-so, or wants a certain kind of sock
- Picky eaters—gets stuck on one certain food and refuses to eat anything else
- Oversensitivity or undersensitivity to smell—may sniff people, objects, food
- Oversensitivity or undersensitivity to sounds— frequently covers ears
- Has an exceptionally high pain tolerance
- Tires easily
- Has an unusually high or low activity level
- Resists new situations

- Has problems with muscle tone, coordination or motor planning

- Can be very impulsive or easily distracted

- Persistently walks on toes to avoid sensory input from the bottom of the feet (this can also be a sign of cerebral palsy if the child is unable to bring his/her feet down flat when asked or when trying)[2]

* * *

Whether you see behavioral red flags in coordination, language, attention, perception or in sensory integration (C.L.A.P.S.), remember that all children learn these behaviors at different rates. Observe your young child over time with other children in their age group; see if they begin to work out some of their behavioral glitches as they are influenced by their peers. Get feedback from your child's preschool and Sunday school teachers, as well as coaches or private instructors (music, dance, etc.). Do they notice some of these behaviors persisting or increasing in your child? If so, seek help from a professional in learning differences (a list of these is included in the appendix). The earlier your child is evaluated, the earlier he or she can begin therapy and remediation, and the more successful his or her academic experience and social life will be.

DISCIPLINE

I can't tell you the number of times I have heard parents say, "I just need to discipline my child more and then all our problems would go away." There is some truth to the importance of discipline, but parents of a learning-different child quickly find out that their child's behavior problems are not a motivational issue. You can't discipline the brain's neurons. Let me give you some examples.

Tyler

Five-year-old Tyler loved to go to the store with his mother. Almost every time she took him, though, he wanted a toy. Being a typical mother on a budget, she usually said no to Tyler's requests. Every time she said no, Tyler started to scream and throw a temper tantrum, so she immediately took him home to sit in his timeout chair. He sat on that chair for maybe 40 seconds and then raced around the house, drawing the other siblings into his drama.

By this time, Mom was at her wit's end and thankful when Dad came from work. After Dad was brought up to speed on the situation, he went down to Tyler's eye level and told him what the punishment would be for his bad behavior: Tyler would continue to sit on the timeout chair until the timer went off, and there would be no dessert after dinner.

This news brought on an outburst so disturbing that the other children were frightened, an outburst that lasted until Tyler was exhausted. He fell asleep in his timeout chair, so Dad picked him up and put him to bed. The next day, Tyler's behavior was better, but the day after that, Tyler again threw a fit, this time over a toy both he and his brother wanted. Mom and Dad handled that situation in the same way as before, with similar results.

Discipline was not addressing Tyler's pattern of behavior.

Andrew

Andrew was six and had a great friend down the street. His friend just discovered bad words, and shared them with all his friends on the playground. Andrew began using these words around his house, much to the dismay of his mother. She decided to wash Andrew's mouth out with soap every time he used one of these words.

Children who are not learning-different would stop this behavior after tasting that soap the first time. But not Andrew. He was at the sink on a regular basis. After weeks of the same punishment, he said to his mother matter-of-factly, "I really would prefer Camay."

Emma

Emma was a sweet child of seven. She rarely had temper tantrums, but she always seemed to be in a world of make-believe with her dolls and toys. Since she was four or five, her mother noticed that Emma had a passive-resistant attitude. When she asked Emma to do anything, her daughter ignored her and did just as she pleased. This especially aggravated Emma's mother when they were in a hurry to go somewhere.

One day when they were getting ready to leave for school, she asked Emma to get her shoes and socks on, get her lunch and get into the car. Emma's mother waited for her in the car, but Emma never came out. Aggravated and worried that they would be late, Emma's mom raced into the house and found her daughter on the floor of her room with one sock on, playing with a doll. Emma's mom lost her temper and Emma was punished for disobeying. She was told that she would not be able to watch TV or have playmates over that afternoon. Her mother grabbed all the necessary items and they left for school.

* * *

Young children with learning differences who cause chaos in the house on a regular basis are responding to a neurological misfire in their brains. Outbursts cause the chemical levels to rise in their brains so that they can wake to attend the world around them.

This behavior looks different as the child matures. When they get into first and second grades, they may have difficulty staying seated to do simple tasks. When they begin their upper elementary years, they may exhibit destructive behaviors on the playground or act as the class clown.

However much it may look as if Tyler, Andrew and Emma were being willfully disobedient, rebellion was not their motivation. In fact, all three of them may have *wanted* to act appropriately and do what was expected of them. Their "bad" behavior was a manifestation of their learning differences, and traditional discipline could not help them.

That does not mean that learning-different children should not be disciplined; not at all! In fact, consistent discipline is a very important part of raising children with learning differences. But parents must learn how to discipline appropriately and in such a way that their child reaps the rewards of firm, gentle guidance. This means making it clear to your child that discipline is a result of your love.

Love is the most intimate of topics. Most parents, when asked if they love their child, would say without hesitation, "Of course!" But I think the more pertinent question is, "*How* do you love your child?" Are you the kind of parent who yells to get your point across? Are you the kind of parent who says, "I love you," but is too busy with work to spend time with your child? Or are you the kind of parent who is able to speak gentle words of love and affirmation to your child while firmly guiding him or her toward positive behaviors?

> Consistent discipline is a very important part of raising children with learning differences.

Jesus told His followers that *love* is the Greatest Commandment (see Matt. 22:34-40). Yet "love" is a word so overused in our society that I wonder if we even know what it means anymore. We "love" pizza. We "love" to shop. We "love" baseball.

The way we differentiate our "love" for these things and our love for our family is through *action*, both big and small. My father made a point every day to tell all four of us kids and our mother that he loved us. He'd ask, "Hey, Maren . . . did I tell you I love you today?"

Whether he had or not, my response as a small child was always, "Nooooo . . ."

"Well, I do," he'd say, as he wrapped me in a big hug. As we grew older, it became a game to see who could say it first. As adults we still say it to each other, and we have carried the habit into our own families. My father's simple words paired with simple action were his way of obeying Christ's command in our family, and demonstrated to us how we could do the same.

Another way to keep love at the forefront of your family is laughter. Laughter is the music of the soul, and learning to tell the difference between situations that call for discipline and those that need a good belly laugh will allow you and your child to make beautiful music together. Don't take yourself too seriously; when you or your child make a mistake stemming from a learning difference, sometimes it's okay to laugh about it and move on to the next challenge. When you can laugh as a family, joy will be the norm in your home.

TIPS FOR EFFECTIVE DISCIPLINE

With the supreme importance of love in mind, here are 10 tips for disciplining your child effectively.

1. Don't Yell

Yelling will only activate the learning-different part of the brain, which is always seeking stimuli to wake itself up. Instead of making the situation better, yelling is likely to exacerbate your child's inappropriate behavior. This, obviously, will cause you even more aggravation and frustration.

Instead of raising your voice, be the parent and demonstrate some self-control. The more calm you are, the more your child will learn how to deal effectively with conflict in his or her own life.

2. Get on His Level

Bend down to your child's level and hold eye contact. State what you want him to do twice, and then have him repeat your instructions. When it's clear that he knows what you want him to do, release him to accomplish the task.

This approach clarifies what you expect without ridicule or anger, and shows that you respect your child's ability to accomplish what is expected. Using this method will also help your child become more confident in himself and his abilities, and isn't that the goal?

3. Make a Homework Contract
Draw up a homework contract (see example on the following page) signed by you, your child and your child's teacher. This should include specifics about expectations, rewards and penalties. When everyone knows what is expected, conflict can be avoided. Your child will also feel more secure and confident in her ability to complete assigned work.

4. Make a Behavior Contract
Draw up a behavior contract (see examples on the following pages) signed by you, your child and your child's teacher that sets limits for your child at home and at school. Boundaries are important for all children, but learning-different children especially thrive when they are bounded by secure limits. In particular, children with AD/HD can sometimes feel frightened by their own impulses and will feel safe and empowered when adult authority is firmly established.

5. Reward Immediately
We all want rewards for a job well done, and kids are no different. Don't put him off when he has achieved something; don't think that you'll take care of it later and he'll just have to be patient. Be consistent and give him his reward immediately. His new, positive behavior will become a habit in no time.

HOMEWORK CONTRACT[3]

Week of _____ to _____

+ = Homework complete and on time
X = Homework not available, incomplete or not satisfactory

	Monday	Tuesday	Wednesday	Thursday	Friday
1st hour					
2nd hour					
3rd hour					
4th hour					
5th hour					
6th hour					
Advisory					
Teacher initial					
Parent initial					
Student initial					

Comments_____

Reward _____

Consequences _____

BEHAVIOR CONTRACT FOR HOME

Behavior	Reward	Consequence
Clean room by the time you leave for school	$5.00 per week	Do not receive allowance
Do dishes three nights a week	$5.00 per week	Do not receive allowance
Take out the trash and do yard work	$5.00 per week	Do not receive allowance
Lying		Grounded for two weeks
Bad attitude		Computer taken away for one week
Fighting with siblings		No TV for one week

Student Signature _____

Date _____ / _____ / _____

Parent Signature _____

Date _____ / _____ / _____

(This example is for an older child, but it can be modified to meet your particular need.)

BEHAVIOR CONTRACT FOR SCHOOL[4]

(At the top, list specific behaviors that are acceptable and unacceptable for your child in the classroom. This will vary depending on your child's age, so work with his or her teacher[s] to establish these guidelines.)

Week of _____ to _____

+ = Acceptable classroom behavior   X = Unacceptable classroom behavior

	Monday	Tuesday	Wednesday	Thursday	Friday
1st hour					
2nd hour					
3rd hour					
4th hour					
5th hour					
6th hour					
Advisory					
Teacher initial					
Parent initial					
Student initial					

Comments_____

Reward _____

Consequences _____

6. Encourage Positive Behavior

It is human nature to focus on the negative. Look at the evening news! If only positive stories were reported, how many of us would bother watching? When it comes to discipline, however, nothing beats catching your child doing something right. Affirming and rewarding positive behavior lets her know what to do instead of what *not* to do. As a bonus, when you focus on the positive, you become more positive yourself. And when Mom is happy, everybody's happy!

7. Tell Him Why You Like and Love Him

How often do you tell your child that you love and like him? Society tells us to love all kinds of ridiculous things: our wardrobe, our cars, our houses, our friends, and so on. But what about our kids? Too often, our culture tells parents to work to get more stuff to love, and give their children more stuff to love, too.

Don't fall for it. Make sure your child knows how unconditional your love is for him, and demonstrate it with an investment of your time and attention. Tell him specifically why you like him, and do it on a regular basis. When he knows how treasured he is, he'll be ready for whatever struggle comes along.

8. Remind Her that God Has Given Her Special Talents

How often were you encouraged to do something with your life based on a unique and special gift? Not very often? If you still believe that little voice in your head that says, "You're not good enough" or "You can't do that; it's too hard," how can your child have any hope for her future? Don't let lies be your legacy. It's time to break that cycle of negativity and let God's gifts shine in your family.

Be specific when you talk to your child about her gifts and talents, and encourage her to be creative in thinking about how to use them. Encourage her faith in God by letting her take risks and go through open doors, and remind her that failure is part of the process . . . not a reason to quit.

9. Nourish His Dreams

Learning-different children, especially those with AD/HD, have the ability to see the big picture, and this is a tremendous gift to humanity. When they dream, they dream big. Don't squelch this in your child; dreaming is a part of who he is. Do your best to understand your child's goals and help him plan to make them a reality. Don't miss out. Encourage greatness!

10. Be Consistent

Consistency is difficult for every parent, but it is especially hard for adults with AD/HD. And when you add a learning-different child into the mix, the difficulties are magnified. Behavior contracts can be the saving grace, because expectations, rewards and consequences are established long before discipline is required. When in doubt, write it down! Then, when expectations are not met, you don't have to think on your feet. You'll know exactly what to do, and can respond to behavioral infractions calmly and consistently.

TIME MANAGEMENT

You don't have to live life like everybody else. Instead, structure your family's life to reflect the reality of learning differences. This may mean adding more routine or making more time for flexibility. Take a long, hard look at your family's daily routine. Talk together about what works and what could be improved, then don't be afraid to make those changes.

Your days do not have to be filled with a thousand different activities. It's not outrageous to choose only one outside activity per child in order to enjoy down-time with each other. Your learning-different child needs time to process the world around her. There is so much outside stimuli demanding her attention; it is imperative to have quiet time to process what her world means. She also needs time to just play and explore her world on her terms. Let's take a look at the Newman family's daily schedule to see what does and doesn't work.

The Newmans are a typical American family. They have three children, two of whom have learning differences with differing severities. Their day looks something like this:

6:30 – Get the children up for school
7:00 – Eat breakfast
7:30 – Leave for school
8:00 – Drop kids off at school
8:30 – Arrive at work
3:45 – Pick kids up at school. Feed children snacks in the car on the way to after-school activities
4:00 – Drop one child at dance class
4:15 – Drop another child at karate class
4:30 – Drop another child at tutoring
4:45 – Pick up one child from dance class
5:00 – Pick up another child from karate
5:15 – Pick up the last child from tutoring

6:00 – Home for the day. Start dinner
6:30 – Dinner on the table
7:00 – Begin homework and help children when needed
9:00 – Hopefully, get the kids to bed
10:00 – Catch breath and get reacquainted with spouse

The one thing the Newman parents have not considered is transitions, which are both important and easily overlooked. Learning-different children often have a hard time transitioning from one activity to the next. On top of that, during school hours, they expend 50 to 75 percent more energy than their peers to accomplish the same work. (Imagine if all the text you have to read looks like German. You have no idea where to begin to decode this language, let alone to comprehend it. All your energy is spent trying to make sense of what is expected, and achievement feels unattainable. When the afternoon bell finally rings, that's your signal to breathe a sigh of relief. The only problem confronting you now is that you have to do it all over again tomorrow.)

With this stress level on a daily basis, learning-different children need some down-time to process their day. This transition must be thoughtfully put together by Mom and Dad. When you pick up the kids, have soothing music playing in the car, or nothing at all. Let your children tell you how their day went on their timetable. Many times, learning-different children have a difficult time articulating their experiences; they can be overwhelmed by their school surroundings and may need some time, without feeling pressured, to communicate what has happened.

When you get home, have a healthy snack ready, then let your child play and blow off some steam. When it is time for homework, give them a 10-minute warning to let them know that they will be transitioning to a new activity. The drama will be minimized with plenty of preparation. Make sure that you have a designated study area that is the same each evening, a place with minimal stimuli that might lead to distraction. Try to avoid fluorescent lighting in the study area; many of these children do not work well in harsh chemical lights. Soft, indirect lighting with lamps is your best bet.

If your child is having a hard time sitting still long enough to complete his work, use a timer. Set the timer for 15 minutes, and when the timer goes off allow your child a 5-minute break to expend his extra energy. When the timer goes off again, have him go back to work for another 15 minutes.

Now let's get real! It's a rare day that goes perfectly according to schedule, even if you make every effort to flexibly plan for transitions. Even when there are no learning differences thrown into the mix, the unexpected is bound to happen, and all the more so when learning differences are a daily part of your child's life. He may be over-stimulated, may have a conflict with a peer or teacher at school or may do poorly in class, and any one of these can lead to stress and miscommunication between parents and children. Don't be surprised if you occasionally have an emotional meltdown on your hands. When and if it happens, be the calm amidst the storm. Don't add to your child's frenetic over-stimulation by letting your emotions run wild, too. When you respond with compassionate calm, it won't be long until your child can take a deep breath (or two) and rebound from the trying time he has experienced. And even though you are almost certain to deal with occasional emotional highs and lows, a flexible routine can help to minimize the impact of these outbursts.

As you set reachable, realistic behavioral goals for your child; calmly, consistently respond with rewards and consequences; and find a schedule that makes the most of your family's time together, your child will be well on the way toward success and security in his or her academic, home and social life.

5

Making Sense of Adolescence

It is important to realize your teen's strengths. Teenagers with AD/HD and other learning differences are usually a joy to have around. They are often funny and creative. They are not afraid to try new things and have a zest for life that the rest of the world too often lacks.

When parents first meet with me about their teen's learning difference, one of the first questions that comes up is, "What will become of him? What will his future hold?" Obviously, I do not know. Each child is different in his personal motivations and each family comes with varied and special dynamics. The one question I *can* answer is, "Have other children with similar differences succeeded in college and beyond?"

Of course they have! Some have chosen to go on to college, with all its challenges, while others have chosen trade school and gone on to be very successful in their lives. So much depends on the family's need to stay in the Sea of Denial or its willingness to move on, guiding their child toward a world of adventure and happiness. This begins when parents can take a long look at their teen's strengths instead of his or her weaknesses.

Strengths at Home/ Community	Strengths at School
• Intelligent	• Intelligent
• Creative	• Good with computers
• Great sense of humor	• Always interested in current events
• Always willing to help others	• Loves to debate
• Sensitive	• Complies with rules
• Willing to take medication	• Does his work well
• Pursues outside interests	• Is a good writer
	• Enjoys science

Name _____   Age _____
Grade _____

By starting with your teenager's strengths, I don't mean to give the impression that the difficulties you experience with your learning-different teen are minimal or nonexistent. But I do hope you realize that your child has been created by God with a unique set of traits, gifts and strengths. He or she is no accident. Yes, parenting him or her through adolescence will not always be a walk in the park, but remembering what he or she has to offer to the world can put your high calling into perspective.

DIAGNOSIS

Often times, undiagnosed teens have coped very well through their early years. Because of their high IQs, they are often able to figure out what is expected of them by observation. As they get older, however, the quantity of information becomes so great that their coping mechanisms are overwhelmed. Before a parent gets an accurate diagnosis of their learning-different teen, they may go through some really rough waters. Undiagnosed AD/HD teens often experience rather sudden difficulty in school and social relationships and may feel overwhelmed by the simplest tasks. A majority of teens occasionally experience similar difficulties as they navigate the waters of adolescence, but if these problems persist over time, then it is a good idea to get your teen tested for possible learning differences. (There is a list of testing centers across the nation in the Resources section of this book.)

I am a firm believer in the accuracy and helpfulness of the testing methods currently in use. These have been developed and continue to evolve using the best and newest research into AD/HD and other learning differences. It is a good rule of thumb to get a complete battery of tests, including The Wechsler Intelligence Scale (third or fourth edition); the Woodcock-Johnson III Test of Cognitive Ability; the Woodcock-Johnson III Tests of Achievement; Gray Oral Reading Tests, Fourth Edition (GORT-4); the Berea-Gestalt Test of Motor Perception; the Quick Neurological Screening Test, Revised Edition (QNST-R); and the Behavior Assessment System for Children, Second Edition (BASC-2). It usually takes a full day to complete these tests, so be wary if a doctor just asks 40 questions and then gives a diagnosis. (This happens more often than you'd think.)

I am also an enthusiastic proponent of SPECT (Single Photo Emission Computer Tomography) scanning, mentioned in chapter 1, which pinpoints areas in the brain affected by

AD/HD. This scan, coupled with the traditional testing mentioned above, can give a more accurate and thorough diagnosis. SPECT by itself is not strictly a diagnostic tool; it simply clarifies learning differences that are typically difficult to pinpoint. This kind of diagnostic accuracy cannot be replicated in any other way.

I first encountered SPECT scanning at the Amen Clinics when we had trouble finding the right medication to treat our youngest daughter. We were playing "let's try this, now that," and it was a frustrating experience, not least for her. That's when I discovered that Dr. Amen, using SPECT scanning, can see the brain in three dimensions while the brain works on a concentration activity. The scan shows areas of the brain that are under-stimulated or over-stimulated during a variety of activities.

Sure enough, the scans showed that Alicia's anxiety, stemming from her problems with auditory processing, was not being touched by her current medication. It also showed that she had ADD, a fact that had not been picked up in any other testing. Parts of her brain were firing too hot, like a solar flare on the sun. She needed those areas calmed before her ADD medication could be effective, and the Amen Clinic was able to give us holistic options as well as traditional medications to treat her particular situation. Today, Alicia is a different person because of that scan. Her medications are working well and she is experiencing success in all areas of her life.

After Alicia's success, we decided to have the whole family scanned. (My husband, Bob, suggested that we take down our family portrait from the wall and put up our brain scans instead.) It was incredible to see how each person's learning difference showed up so clearly. Jackie, Alicia's older sister, had similar "hot" areas, but hers were less pronounced. She, too, needed medication to calm the areas of over-stimulation. Nick's scan, on the other hand, showed hardly any activity in his cerebellum, a clear indication that stimulation was needed to "wake up" that area of his brain. (Without Nick's SPECT scan, we might have floundered for years, trying one medication after another only to watch him suffer severe side effects, including heart palpitations resulting from stimulants. Being able to pinpoint Nick's particular kind of ADD—different from both his sisters'—meant that we could narrow down the list of medicines that would help him and focus even more on behavior modification techniques, which have been the bedrock of his continuing success.)

Seeing these scans made me a believer that SPECT imaging is a wonderful tool for getting a clearer picture of AD/HD and other learning differences and for deciding how to treat them. (Our experience with SPECT imaging also proved the old axiom that every child is different. As parents, we must look at the needs of each child individually and treat him or her accordingly. What is good for one may not be good for the other.)

If you are having difficulty clarifying your child's learning difference, you can read more about Dr. Amen's research at www.amenclinics.com.

MEDICATION

It is not uncommon for undiagnosed AD/HD teens to self-medicate with alcohol or drugs, seeking a place where they feel "normal." The drugs of choice for AD/HD individuals are usually alcohol first and then cocaine. These substances push neurotransmitter levels over their normal range for a period of time. Because of their typically low levels of neurotransmitters such as dopamine, norepinephrine and serotonin, people with AD/HD are easily addicted to these mood-enhancing substances.

Below is a closer look at what behaviors are affected when an individual's brain gets too much or too little of particular neurotransmitters:

NEUROTRANSMITTERS AND RELATED BEHAVIORS[2]

	High Level	Low Level
Norepinephrine Dopamine	• Thrill seeking • Seeks new activities • Impulsive aggression	• Indifferent • Depressed • Planned aggression
Serotonin	• Undistracted • Works intensely on tasks • Satisfaction • Sense of wellbeing • Focus on one thing • Helps with sleep	• Inattentive • Distractible, moves from one thing to another • Difficulty completing a job • Difficulty thinking ahead • Difficulty delaying response • Cognitive impulsivity • Dissatisfaction/ irritability • Aggression toward self or others • Impulsivity • Difficulty sleeping • Setting fires • Obsessive-compulsive • Suicide risk

If your child is experimenting with drugs, his body is trying to regulate his brain's neuro-transmitter levels. When the chemical levels of serotonin, norepinephrine and dopamine are brought up to a normal level, even for a short period of time, the child feels "normal," possibly for the first time in his life. And that's a great place to be! Unfortunately, the dangers that accompany substance abuse are not great at all.

That is why it is extremely important to get the right medication for your child's learning difference if you think that the diagnosis warrants it. With the right medication at the right dose administered under a doctor's care, a learning-different teen or adult can have the peaceful and productive life that God intends for them.

It is important to find the right doctor to go down this path with you. It is best if you can find a neurologist or a psychiatrist who specializes in treatments for

Random Polls

If your child has ever taken prescription medication for AD/HD, did you . . .

32% Find a medication that worked well on the first try?

34% Find a medication that worked well after two or three tries?

11% Find a medication that worked well after four or more tries?

10% Give up trying to find a medication that worked well?

10% Other

If your child takes medication for AD/HD, does she take any regular breaks from the medication?

52% No, she takes medications every day.

5% Yes, she takes breaks on weekends and/or holidays.

7% Yes, she takes a break over the summer.

27% Yes, she takes a break on weekends and/or holidays, and over the summer.

7% Yes, she takes occasional breaks from medication at times other than those above.[3]

children and adults with AD/HD. These specialists are trained to administer the correct and effective dosage of medication to your child. Family doctors and pediatricians, on the other hand, do not usually have the in-depth training required to understand appropriate drug therapies for learning-different people. The old saying "A little bit of information can be deadly" is very true in this instance. It is also extremely important for parents to do research on their own, rather than trusting TV personalities or pharmaceutical advertising for guidance.

There is still such controversy over whether or not to medicate children with learning differences in order for them to be successful in school and beyond. I struggled with this dilemma. It took me a long time to put even one of my children on medication. I lived in the pride current of the Sea of Denial for about two years; I did not want anyone to judge me or my child. Eventually, however, we gave it a month-long trial. That month was the first time in her life that my daughter found success. Once her serotonin levels were within a normal range, everything seemed to fall into place for her.

Many of my teen and adult clients have told me that when they were finally given proper medication under a doctor's care, it helped to calm their heads. When I ask them to explain, many of them use the following analogy: "When I don't have my medication, my brain is like a train coming down the tracks at a hundred miles an hour. I want to see all the scenery along the way, but everything is moving so fast that my surroundings are a blur. Then I know that we're coming into the station and I want to get off, but the train just won't stop. And when I do try to get off, teachers and parents get upset with me and don't understand why I act the way that I do.

When I take my medication, though, the train moves at a smooth pace. I am able to see all the scenery and I enjoy it. When I see the station coming up, I prepare myself to get off. Getting on and off of the train is easy." If your child is like so many others with learning differences, medication, in conjunction with other remediation therapies, may help them in a similar way. Remember, medications are simply a tool; they are not a cure. But they can be one of the most important tools your child uses to forge future success.

ENSURING YOUR TEEN'S SUCCESS

Learning-different teens can benefit from AD/HD coaching. A coach is a professional who is trained in methods to guide them through life skills, which can be a tremendous help if the teen is willing to be the leader of her support team. They sit down with the teen and find out what her goals are and then help her plan ways to achieve those goals. They help organize her homework time and workspace and teach her effective study skills, all things she needs to succeed in school. They can also stay in touch with the student's teacher to make sure that she is achieving her goals. If the coach is also trained in language and speech therapy, he or she can help the student with remedial work.

Next, make sure that you and your teen have a great support system. This means working together as a family to help each other get through this rocky time. Don't play the blame game; move out of that current and focus on the unique gifts and talents within your family. Make sure that you provide a good church environment for your family, because God must

Random Polls
How much time per week do you spend driving your kids around?

16% 0 to 2 hours

20% 3 to 4 hours

24% 5 to 6 hours

15% 7 to 8 hours

23% 9 hours or more

be the center of your teen's life. Your teen may not act as if it is important, but deep down these traditions will give him the anchor he needs throughout his life. Be consistent with church activities and surround yourself and your child with people who hold to like-minded values. God will not forsake you if you are raising His child as He desires.

Communication is also key for you and your teen. Commit yourself to take at least 30 minutes a night to have a meaningful talk with him. In our house, we do it two different ways. We go up before they go to sleep and sit on their beds to ask how their days were. If you do the same, your teen may be surprised. He may even say, "I don't need to be tucked in anymore, Mom." But just begin and watch what happens; he will come to value that quiet time with you more and more. We also take time in the car, both in the mornings and after school. In the morning, we have an opportunity to set the pace for the day, and in the afternoon, we can debrief their day at school while it's still fresh in their minds. Whether he tells you or not, your teen will love that you talk to him and want to hear what's on his mind. Make time in the car your time together. He will grow up all too soon, so value and treasure him while you have a chance.

Another important milestone in your teen's life is getting her first job and managing her money. Mastering a good work ethic and wise money management before she moves on to college is imperative. As we discussed in earlier sections, learning-different children have a difficult time comprehending inferences, which make relationships difficult. Without remediation, this will be true in the work place. It is important that you guide your teen into a job where she will succeed, which will give her experience in time management, teamwork and people skills. There are some jobs that would not be good choices for this formative experience. For example, sending your AD/HD teen to work in a toy store is probably not wise; there are too many distractions, from the quantity and variety of products to be stocked, to the noise and activity. Guide your teen toward a work experience that will confirm her ability to succeed.

Managing money is often difficult for those with AD/HD and some other learning differences. Because of impulsiveness, these individuals are often perpetually broke, so wise money management should be mastered before high-school graduation. When a teen gets his first paycheck, take him to the bank to open up his first account. Let the new-accounts officer explain all the opportunities that the bank has to offer him, and then help him decide what kind of account is best for his needs. When you get home, ask him to repeat what was said to reinforce what he just learned, then break down the information into smaller pieces to make sure he really understands what is happening with his money. This is also a great time to show him the value of tithing and saving.

Above all, never miss a chance to let your teen know that you are on his or her team. Don't let loneliness or alienation block his or her path to rich relationships and exciting opportunities. Adolescence can be tough for any family, and AD/HD or other learning differences can make it that much tougher.

On the other hand, with proper medication and remediation, good communication and healthy doses of loving respect, you and your teen can grow closer as you journey together.

6

Mom to the Rescue!

God gives mothers a rare and wonderful gift: the gut-level instinct to care for our young. And when our children are threatened in any way, we want to save them. Unfortunately, mothers of learning-different children seem to have an extra helping of that gift. When our children are threatened, we want to lighten their burden by living that burden for them.

I should know; I have done it for my own learning-different children. I made it my solemn vow never to let my children fall through the cracks. I remember when my oldest daughter, Jackie, was eight years old. She had some difficulty with auditory processing as well as ADD, which meant that in social situations, it was very hard for her to pick up inferences from others' body language. She came home one day from school and told me that the other kids would not let her play. When I heard this distressing news, I had the bright idea that I should become the lunch-duty mom so that I could "keep an eye" on what was happening. She was being threatened, and of course it was my duty to protect her from all things great and small.

I was also very good at "helping" with homework. I think I've passed first through eighth grades twice now; too bad I don't have the paperwork to prove it. I can't tell you the number of times my learning-different children came to me in tears, sobbing that they just didn't understand what they were supposed to do for homework, and the test in history is tomorrow and they forgot their book and spiral at school. The mothering instinct part of me always stood up to the challenge: "Don't worry, dear; we will work this out." Actually, I was really saying, "Don't worry, dear; I will fix this for you."

I have been known to go to the school after hours and get the janitor to open the building so that I could retrieve the necessary materials. I have also been known to call most every parent in my child's class to get homework assignment directions. We (my child and I) would then sit down to complete the job of homework and test studying. My child would always start out great, with the best of intentions, but then after a mere hour he or she would break into tears, saying, "I'm so tired. I can't do this anymore." By the time the last two pages of homework were still incomplete, they had fallen asleep at the table. After putting them to bed, I would return to finish their homework for them, often working until midnight (after which I went to bed and cried my eyes out, wondering what would become of us). All that work, only to find out the next day that my special sweetie had forgotten everything he or she had studied the night before and had gotten a 32 percent on the history test. Oh, yes, and the homework had mysteriously disappeared between our house and the school. This was often followed by a phone call from the teacher to let me know that my child needed to study more and get more organized. The conversation usually ended with the teacher saying, "You know, you really should be more involved with your child's study habits."

And then there were the times when teachers told me that medication might help my children stay on task. My response was always, "Thank you for your interest in my child, but my husband and I will take care of it." In reality, if I had told Bob that the school had suggested medication for our children, he would have said they were crazy. It was my quest never to medicate my child. I was determined to take all sugar and artificial coloring out of their diets; I was convinced that would "cure" everything. The homework misadventures continued and my children's social lives were not improved by what they ate, but I was convinced I had conquered learning differences.

I had a rude awakening one afternoon when my older daughter came home from school and said that there was to be a spelling test the next day. Jackie wanted to get her homework done and go out to play, so we sat down to tackle those words. She fidgeted and rolled around on the floor as I dictated the words to her. I kept asking her to sit still so that we could finish, but she wouldn't (or couldn't). I finally found myself sitting on her feet to keep her still. I realized how ridiculous I must look and how humiliated my daughter must be. *What was I doing?* At that moment, I wondered if medication might really help her. My husband and I talked it over and decided to give it a trial for one month. If there were no difference, then we would take Jackie off of it.

Boy, did it ever make a difference! She was able to focus at school. Her grades went from Cs and Ds to As and Bs. She was relaxed and relieved, and I realized that I had been depriving my daughter of something her body really needed. (As I prepared to write this chapter, I called Jackie at college to ask what she remembered of that time in our lives. It was funny; I remember it all as if it were yesterday, but her reply was, "All I remember, Mom, is how great I felt when I finally got on my medicine. My life seemed to begin then.")

MOTHERING GOD'S WAY

Sometimes a mother's instinct is not actually what is best for our child. We need to fine-tune our instincts to God's desires for us. We must surrender ourselves and our children to Him; otherwise, our pride shows its ugly face once again.

In my need to rescue my children from the alienation and heartache that seemed destined to be theirs, I chose to step in too far. My life became enmeshed with theirs. I couldn't tell where their life-experiences ended and mine began. When friends invited us to go places, I always wondered how it would affect the children. Finally, my son said one day, "Mom, I kind of want to go on the campout myself. Is that okay?" At that moment, I realized that I was living their lives for them, and that was not healthy.

> We need to fine-tune our instincts to God's desires for us.

I finally had the courage to step back and let God begin to run my family. I began to pray through the day, asking God to guide me as I parented these children. As I did, I began to see what needed to be done.

First, I mourned the loss of what I thought my children might miss. I didn't know if they would be able to experience the great things in life that I had. Would they have long-lasting friendships with their peers? Would they make the honor roll or get asked to the prom by the popular boy or girl? Would they make it to the college of their choice and be able to graduate? Would they find a spouse who would understand their learning differences and have a successful marriage? The idea that they might miss out weighed heavily on my heart, and that is what motivated my need to control their lives. I was not *guiding* them through life; I was *controlling* them through life.

Next, I sat down with my children individually and asked, "If you could do or be anything in the world, what would it be?" I was amazed at their detailed answers. Their dreams and goals were beautiful, and much better than anything I could have thought up for them. Then I decided to stand next to them and guide them, rather than thinking I was leading when I was actually standing in their way. We took a long look at their dreams and goals and worked backward, figuring out what they needed to do today to get where they wanted to go. We began to work as a family, as a team.

Another great blessing was finding a school where they could thrive. My husband was transferred to the Dallas area, and I came kicking and screaming from Los Angeles. I loved the beach and our family was in L.A., and here we were in the middle of nowhere (or so I thought). It was all in God's perfect plan. A friend told me about a school that works with learning-different children, and I walked on campus one day to see what it was like. I was truly amazed. The kids were all interacting with each other, laughing and enjoying themselves, and the teachers seemed to really love the kids. The Shelton School has been part of our lives for many years now, and it will forever be a part of our hearts. (If you do not live in the Dallas-Fort Worth area, don't worry: You'll find information in the Resources section about other schools across the nation that specialize in learning differences.)

As the mother of a learning-different child, let your God-given instincts lead you to what is truly best for your precious child. Ask God to show you how to be the mother your child needs. Mourn the loss of what you had hoped for him. Find out what your child's dreams and goals are, and work backward to make them a reality. Finally, find the right school where he will thrive. As you walk beside your child and guide him toward God's calling for his life, you will be the mother God intended all along.

7

Where's Dad?

Fathers are the best-kept secret in a world that tells us the traditional family unit is not worth much anymore. Dads are the guiding forces behind great men and valued women in the next generation.

Fathering is also one of the most difficult jobs in the world. Think about it: Dads are usually there by our sides when we give birth; they are our cheerleaders as their offspring come into the world. At the moment our child takes her first breath, it becomes his job to provide for and protect her until he takes his last breath. Women brag about how we handled our pain anywhere from 6 to 36 hours, and we're certain that our loving husbands could never handle it. In reality, they handle it in a different way for years and years. They work their hearts out, sacrificing their lives for their families on a daily basis. If we are wise, we will never buy into the lie our culture sells us; instead, we must value the self-sacrificing love that can only come from a devoted father.

Dads often have a difficult time adjusting to the reality of a learning-different child. They have a strong tendency toward denial. They are often not around their child as much as the mother, and so don't have the opportunity to observe their child's learning difference in action. They are also sometimes inclined to chalk up their wives' concern about behavior problems to overreaction. For example, if Johnny comes home with a note from the teacher that says, "Johnny threw a spit ball in class and will have to stay after school tomorrow," Dad's reaction might be, "Boys will be boys." Mom's reaction, on the other hand, might be, "What is causing Johnny to throw spitballs?" Mom will analyze this for hours, while Dad has moved on to the next problem to be solved.

Because of these tendencies, admitting and adjusting to learning differences in their children can become a long and drawn-out process for fathers. When a family first suspects that there might be a learning difference, it is usually the mother who picks up on the minute symptoms that are emerging. When Mom comes to Dad with her suspicions, Dad's reaction is that Mom is overreacting; Susie is just a kid . . . she will grow out of the behavior. So they take a wait-and-see attitude. Mom doesn't want to rock the boat, so her balancing act continues

> We must value the self-sacrificing love that can only come from a devoted father.

between school, home and the child, and she becomes more and more reluctant to mention the red flags she sees. Meanwhile, Dad thinks everything is fine.

Many families stay stuck in this spot for years, and that means Susie stays stuck too, losing remediation time by the day. Once again, as her parents swirl around in the Sea of Denial, it is the child who loses out.

Let me give you some real-life examples of families who have gone through this pattern. The first family stayed in the denial phase for only a short time. The second family stayed in this phase for seven years.

THE REDDING FAMILY

The Reddings are a wonderful family with two children. Their older child was screened for a possible learning difference when he was in the first grade. Joey was having trouble identifying letters and decoding the written word. There was also some concern about his auditory processing.

Dad was a neurologist and wanted a conference the minute the screening was complete. The teachers and specialists were all present as we shared the news with Mom and Dad: Joey was just wired a little differently. There were signs of auditory processing disorder and dyslexia. Dad was so thorough, trying to understand this by questioning and doing his own research. By the week's end, both Mom and Dad were on board with the therapy we had suggested. Joey was taken out of class twice a week for the SEE (Sequential English Education) Program and twice a week for auditory processing remediation with a speech therapist.

Joey worked through his remediation for two years and is now thriving in school. As he grows and matures, he will have times in his life when he might have some difficulty with his written expression, but the Redding family can return for follow-up visits with a learning-different therapist to help. Joey will always have dyslexia and auditory processing disorder, but he is learning to use different pathways in his brain to achieve the goals of reading and listening.

It would be wonderful if all parents reacted as swiftly as the Redding family.

THE HOBART FAMILY

Mr. and Mrs. Hobart married a little later in life. It was a second marriage for Dad and the first for Mom. Dad had two grown children from his previous marriage. Now he and his wife had two children of their own, who were 16 and 8.

Mom hired me to "help" their eight-year-old, Noah, with his homework because he had been diagnosed with oral language disorder and dyslexia. There had been previous attempts at remediation, but the language therapist who had begun to work with Noah was transferred out of state. Mom had dropped the ball by not finding someone else to replace her immediately. Instead, she found "programs" advertised on television or through catalogs that promised the same results. None of them worked.

Noah began to experience severe migraine headaches that took him out of school many days a month. Dad was certain that he just needed to study harder and take medicine for his migraines. This pattern went on for years.

The family used my services as a homework tutor rather than as a therapist to remediate Noah's problems. I carried him through that school year and watched as he struggled with his assignments. The Hobart family eventually found a school for Noah where his learning differences were addressed, but not until he started high school.

BE A FATHER!

Dad, get involved and help your child maneuver through these challenging times. Be a solid, balancing force for your family and don't be afraid to meet the needs of your learning-different child. The trick is to partner with your wife, working as a team to surround your family in security and love. God has given you a mighty task: to nurture and guide His treasures. Joseph, who was chosen to be Jesus' earthly father, must have felt it to be an overwhelming task—but he never gave up. He and Mary worked as a team to raise up their child to His full potential. Their examples must guide us all. Remember, Dad: You are loved and needed.

SECTION THREE

EDUCATING YOUR LEARNING-DIFFERENT CHILD

8

An Education in Schooling

For many learning-different children, school is terrifying. Put yourself in the shoes of these students:

> I am 13 and am scared to death to come to class every day. I look lost, but you call me lazy. I look unprepared, and you think I just don't care. I look bored, but you say I have a bad attitude. You tell my parents that things need to change or I will fail. But I don't even know who I am yet and I don't know how to change. I just wish you would take the time to know who I am and how I learn.

> I am 6. I had a hard time in kindergarten. I try to keep up, but you say I'm much slower than the others in the class and I should hurry up. I don't know why. When I move faster, I don't know what you want me to do next. I feel so sad inside and I don't think you like me. I want to go home. I have a stomachache.

> I am 7 and I can't read very good. I hope you will not call on me to read. I think the whole class will laugh at me. Sometimes I get so scared that my heart hurts and

I think I'm going to die. Can't you see there is something wrong with me? I think you like to see me hurt or you would not call on me.

I am 9 and you tell me I don't try very hard. But I really do. I just forget what I read and I forget what you said, a lot. When I ask you to repeat what you said, you get angry. So I stopped asking. I heard you say to someone else that you would get a paddle and use it if they don't "shape up." Would you use it on me? My dad hits me, too. I thought I was safe here. I'm scared, and I guess you want me to be scared of you. I just want to be safe. Sometimes I don't think I'll live very long.

I am 8 and I talk a lot. I think that if I talk a lot, you won't notice that I can't read or write. But instead you keep putting my name on the board. My mom and dad won't like that, so I think I'll break my pencils instead. Then maybe you'll see that I can't do my work. I feel nervous all the time and I don't know why. I wish you could help me instead of be mad at me.

I am 16 and I feel like everything is out of control. You tell me that I'm so unorganized, but I don't know how to organize. I studied all last night for my algebra test and failed it today. I still don't get it, but you said that you're tired of going over it with me and I have to take responsibility myself. I wonder if I will ever be good at anything. Nothing ever seems to go my way. Will I make it to college? I'm so scared of failing that I don't know how to live.

Finding the right school, with the right teachers, for these children and others like them must be a top priority. Those who choose the vocation of teaching are generally a very caring group of people. The challenges facing them are huge, but there *are* solutions.

As of the writing of this book, I have a very dear friend who is dying with an inoperable brain cancer. She has been a teacher for over 30 years. She taught middle school math in both public and private school. When the news of her illness was first discovered, family and friends where terrified for her prognosis. We all wondered how we could handle watching the slow grip of death rob her of her faculties. Yet as she came out of her initial brain surgery, her attitude was amazing. She put God front and center, as she had throughout her life. She believed that this path was specifically chosen to bring her even closer to her beloved God. She used what the world might perceive as the most horrible situation to show us all that the world was wrong.

In the weeks that followed, she received cards and letters from students she had taught over the years. Each one reflected the same message, in different words: She had changed their lives for the better. She had cared enough to really listen. She had made them feel as if they really mattered.

Here is my friend's secret:

God has given me the grace to see others as He sees them. Whenever I met a student, I would reflect back their beauty. I can see now that my main job on this earth was to affirm others every day of my life. To affirm another soul, you have to be looking, with genuine honesty and love, and let them know what you see.

I had a student once that failed all of the assessments. She came in for tutoring two times a week and still had difficulty. One day she came to me and said, "You better talk to the boy in the back of the room. Something is terribly wrong. He needs help. I just don't know what it is." I did talk to this student at the end of class and sure enough there were some real problems that he was dealing with. Had she not told me, I don't know where this child would be today. This student could sense that others needed help. She could feel the vibrations in the air when something was wrong. She had a much better gift than math.

She would build people up in her lifetime. I could see this in her and she had to know her gift. I made it a point throughout that year to affirm her gift so that she would know what her path was meant to be. It is so important to recognize all of your students' giftedness and tell them.

I believe that the call of our faith is be to paying attention. The teacher cannot be bound by ego. If they are bound by ego, then they can't focus on the other. God is undistracted when He looks at us. He sees only us, and that penetrates our souls. Unfortunately, there are so many pressures in all areas of our world that we do not see the other. That is a shame. The opportunity to make a difference in the life of a child is magnificent, and if we allow the ego to take over, a soul can be ignored and ultimately lost.

Whatever education route you decide is best for your child, make it your mission to find educators and therapists who share my friend's philosophy. How can a child learn anything when a teacher's facial expression is constantly negative, her physical gestures are intimidating and her language is degrading? Children, learning-different or not, are gifts from God. They deserve educators who recognize their worth and uniqueness and who will strive to make them feel safe and to bring out the best in them. My friend may be a tough act to follow, but there are plenty of incredible teachers and therapists out there who have tender hearts toward God's special children.

With that in mind, let's look at the variety of options available to your child to get the best education possible.

PUBLIC SCHOOLS

Many parents of young learning-different children have placed an unquestionable trust in the public school system, only to learn that the system could only assist them if their child scored below a 16-percent discrepancy on the learning-differences testing. This was shocking enough, but then these parents found out that their child would not be offered special services if he or she were reading within one grade level, even though it is well known that any child not reading at least two grade levels above their grade is likely to struggle. Was their child destined to slip through the cracks?

I can't tell you the number of students that have been brought to me by frustrated parents who have tried to challenge the system. Many have even gone to court to fight for the rights of their children. Of those that have gone to court, only a small percentage have won extra accommodations for their children. In all fairness, the public school system is not funded to help every student with every problem; they must help the most severe with the best services for the least amount of money. Education is a business too, and every business has to budget their funds to stay in business. Unfortunately, it is the children who lose out.

If your child currently attends public school, it is almost certain that you will need the help of an outside therapist or remediation program. Take advantage of the available testing from the public school, but keep in mind that they are testing to see if your child has a 16-percent (or greater) discrepancy between IQ and performance. If he does, the school will receive extra funding. If your student comes in just within this discrepancy, however, your child will be treated as if he has no learning difference. This is the point at which thousands of children fall through the cracks, and that's why it's a good time to ask for a referral to a private diagnostician. There, you can receive information on the educational and therapeutic options that would be most beneficial to your child. You may receive names of private language therapists or speech therapists, depending on individual need.

Look for therapy programs in your area based on the Orton-Gillingham system, which is a multisensory method of education and therapy. All of the student's senses are involved. For example, in the program I use, Sequential English Education (SEE), I remediate spelling errors by using the rough side of a masonite board. Students use the index finger to trace the spelling word three times, and then they write it three times on paper. The trick is that when the student begins to trace the word, he or she must raise his or her elbow and wrist off the table. The sensory input coming from that index finger goes directly to the part of the brain that holds memory, and the child retains the spelling word for that spelling test and beyond. The Wilson Method is another popular multisensory program. It uses a unique "sound tapping" system to help students learn to differentiate the phonemes (speech sounds) in a word. (See this book's Glossary for more information on these and other remediation methods.)

Whatever course you choose for your child, make sure that it is IMSLEC-certified. The International Multisensory Structured Language Education Council is an organization that accredits quality multisensory language courses nationwide. This

---

Random Polls

How does your child feel about his/her school experience this past year?

16% Great
20% Good
25% Okay
10% Disappointed
26% Discouraged

How does your child feel about his/her school experience this past year?

16% Great
19% Good
18% Okay
21% Disappointed
23% Discouraged

How would you rate the school's follow-through on accommodations?

8% Excellent
15% Good
20% Okay
23% Not very good
31% Poor

ensures the quality and effectiveness of the program and those who use it. (More about private therapists can be found later in this chapter.)

Your child can succeed in public school, but don't expect the public system to meet his or her every need. Find out what accommodation is available to your child, and then make up the difference with outside help. Your child is worth it!

PRIVATE SCHOOLS

Private and religious schools have offered quality education for thousands of students for years, and since the explosion of their numbers in the last three decades, they have provided a healthy competition for the public school system. Usually they offer smaller classes and a more demanding curriculum to create more well-rounded and prepared students. Overall, private and religious schools are a great choice for many students.

However, the learning-different child may have a difficult time in this environment. High expectations both academically and socially can create a place where personal success is difficult, if not impossible. Teachers in both public and private schools are typically not qualified to teach a child with learning differences, and as important as smaller class size and student-teacher ratio are for a good education, these are not enough to compensate for learning difficulties.

Too many parents have a blind trust, believing that all teachers can understand and help their child. This is a great mistake. The majority of teachers receive one or two courses under the heading "special education" in college. These courses usually skim various special education needs, including mental retardation, physical handicaps, autism, hearing loss, speech problems and AD/HD. This information may be helpful to teachers trying to identify problems with their students, but it is unlikely to help them remediate problems when they are found.

> The majority of teachers receive one or two courses under the heading "special education" in college.

Parents, do your homework. Even if your child's teacher or a school administrator says that your child will receive special attention for his or her learning differences, get the details. Find out exactly what is planned to accommodate and remediate your child. Do your research and evaluate if these options are right for your child; then consider having the proposed options reviewed by a learning-differences specialist.

Let me tell you the story about Tim, who was a bright student diagnosed with dyslexia and oral language disorder. (Those with expressive language disorder have a very difficult time expressing themselves verbally and in the written word.) Tim was in middle school in a typical private, religious school, and he was having a very hard time making good grades. Some of his assignments were turned in on time and done beautifully, while others were never done at all.

It had been several years since Tim had been given updated testing for his learning differences, so the school principal asked Tim's parents for this. (Schools typically require test updates every three years.) Tim's parents brought the test results to the fall parent-teacher conference, where I was asked to be present as well.

Tim was also required to come to the conference, which must have been terribly daunting for a boy who had severe difficulties reading social cues and facial expressions. When the conference began, each teacher took her turn asking Tim why he was not succeeding in her class. Tim (who was clearly dying inside) looked at each teacher and sincerely promised to do better. Their faces showed that they did not believe him.

The principal chimed in, "Let me see his tests." As he began to look over the documents, I could see that he did not know how to read them; the terminology was completely foreign to him. He finally looked up and asked me to explain the results to the group. (Tim breathed a sigh of relief to no longer be the center of so much negative attention.) As I described how Tim learned best and some ways to help him succeed, I was soon interrupted by one of the teachers: "We don't have time every day to deal with this. We have other students, you know." The conference concluded with Tim being told to work harder. "And we'll have another of these meetings in a couple of months to see how you are doing."

Obviously, the educators at this particular private school were neither trained nor interested in helping Tim succeed in his education. I wish that I could say that this was an unusual scenario, but in my experience, this kind of situation is far from isolated. Because the average teacher receives so little training when it comes to learning differences, *you* must take the initiative.

If you are looking for a private school for your learning-different child, ask these questions:

1. Is this facility equipped to assist or allow outside remediation for a child with learning differences?
2. If so, what are they?
3. Do you offer untimed testing or other accommodations for a child diagnosed with learning differences or who is at risk?
4. Are your teachers educated at all about children with learning differences?
5. If so, what training have they received?
6. Do you offer tutoring?
7. If so, are the tutors allowed to come during the school day?
8. If so, do they offer remediation programs for learning-different students, and what are they?
9. Are any of your teachers trained in courses that are IMSLEC-certified? If so, which courses are they trained to teach?
10. Does your school have a learning lab where a learning-different child can get assistance?

Get in writing what the school has to offer and make sure the principal signs it; you may need this in the future.

Most private and religious schools want to help every student, but as we have discussed, they are not qualified to do so. However, recently at several seminars at which I have presented, I have seen more of an interest from the private sector to get more involved in this area. Unfortunately, it is still only a very few. Educating the educators is still going to take quite some time. Parents, you must be your child's best advocate in his education.

In a perfect world, there would be learning-different schools in every city in the country. Unfortunately, that is not yet the case. There are, however, a growing number of these specialized schools. You can find a list of these in the Resources section of this book.

HOMESCHOOLING

Homeschooling has become the best competition for the traditional educational system here in the United States. Until relatively recently, homeschooling was perceived as something rural folks did when they couldn't afford to educate their child properly. After all, the mother, who had no teaching background, created the curriculum. In the past, there were no guidelines for transcripts or accredited curriculums. But times have definitely changed. Today, traditional education has been forced to sit up and take notice of the new homeschool frontier.

To date, thousands of students have graduated out of the homeschool environment, and 95 percent of that population has gone on to college. They emerge out of this setting with strong social and moral values to become solid citizens. Most homeschool curriculums are accredited in their individual states. Generally, they are well-rounded in their content and many are challenging to their students.

When I first began to homeschool my teenagers, so many of my friends said, "I don't know how you could to that. I could never do that! I don't have the patience to work with my kids all day. I would go crazy!" Another friend told me later that she admired what I was doing and, deep down inside, she envied the time I had with my kids. She admitted that she would love to do the same, but she lacked the confidence in herself to undertake it. This uncertainty seems to be the underlying theme for all new homeschool parents. It is a true leap of faith to go down the homeschooling road, but isn't that what God calls us to do every day?

We chose to homeschool Jackie and Chris through their high school years. Some people suggested that I was trying to protect them from the "evil" world; how would my children be able to function if I took them out of the "real world"? Yet the truth was exactly opposite: Homeschooling was the best preparation available for them to succeed in the "real world." Jackie began to get job offers for her music, and if she was to take advantage of those opportunities, it meant that she would fall behind in her studies at a traditional school. When my husband and I presented homeschooling as an option, she jumped at the chance. When Chris overheard, he said, "Hey, I want to do that, too." Honestly, I was shocked that Chris was interested. But, as I said in the introduction, he knew what he wanted to do and saw that homeschooling could help him get there.

So now we were off to the races, and I was about to have the experience of a lifetime. I chose to work with the School of Tomorrow curriculum, and it proved to be the best for my kids. This program had team teachers assigned to each family who took care of transcripts and all record-keeping. All of my kids' work was accredited through the state, and when it came time to apply for college, they were ready to go and very competitive with their peers.

The one question I was asked again and again was how my children would get social interaction. How ridiculous! Did they think that Chris and Jackie were staying in their rooms, locked up for years? Hardly. Our days looked something like this:

- Up, dressed and ready to go by 9:00 A.M.
- Work on 20 textbook pages per subject per day. Math and science were taught on Tuesday and Thursday by a teacher on maternity leave.
- Complete lessons by 1:00 P.M.
- Lunch as a family by 1:30 P.M.
- Jackie had music (voice and piano) from 2:00 to 4:00 P.M. on Monday, Wednesday and Friday.
- Chris worked from 2:00 to 8:00 P.M. four days a week.
- Jackie worked 2:00 to 8:00 P.M. on Tuesday, Thursday and Saturday.

They found plenty of people with whom to socialize. Their "real world" experience, doing what they dreamed of doing, prepared them to be self-confident for the long haul of life.

I am often asked why we didn't homeschool the younger two. Simple: Each child is different. Just because one child did it doesn't mean it's good for all of them. Nick and Alicia have thrived at Shelton.

Homeschooling may be the most effective way for your learning-different child to find success. The one-on-one instruction is invaluable, and lessons can be tailored to your child's primary learning style. Remember that learning-different students need repetitions of information (at least 1,500 times in their area of weakness) to fully master the concept. These repetitions can come in the form of written, oral, tactical or verbal expression. A child who does not have a learning difference only needs to have repetition of information 50 to 100 times to master a concept. This repetition is easily built in to a home-school curriculum.

Additionally, if a student fails a test, many of the home-school curriculums will not let the student move on. They are required to master the topic and test again. In traditional education, if the student fails a test, they simply get a failing grade and move on to the next material. (Is this effective learning? I don't think so.)

Private learning-different therapists are also available during the day, when your child is fresher and greater gains can be made. If your child needs remediation in certain areas, provide that outside of the daily curriculum. Have a certified therapist come to your home to work with the child for at least three days a week.

Homeschool students are exposed to more types of experiences with a wider variety of age groups than their counterparts. This is very important for the learning-different

Random Polls

How often do you attend conferences or workshops about learning issues?

43% As often as I can. I always learn something new.

23% Sometimes, if it's convenient and the topic is interesting.

28% Rarely/never. I get my information from other sources.

3% Other

child. Usually, homeschool families plug in to a local homeschool organization within their community, which sets up a myriad of activities for all age groups. What's great is that you have like-minded people with like-minded values, working together to guide the next generation. In addition, these groups often encourage community service, such as helping an elderly couple in the neighborhood with their yard work.

Teen students might decide to go to work when they turn 16, and because they are homeschooled, they are able to work longer hours and learn business hands-on, rather than wait until college graduation. These individuals have better social skills for life than do children coming from a traditional school setting.

Overall, the homeschool experience can be a great choice for the learning-different child, but it takes a parent who is not afraid to jump in and educate him- or herself on the various curriculums.

The Angelicum Curriculum

These studies are rigorous, but if you have a high-functioning learning-different child, this might be a fit because you can move at your own pace. This curriculum is a liberal education program based on the classical great books of Western civilization (with optional Socratic discussion seminars). If you enroll in the Great Books program, your child will graduate with 48 college credits. This is one of the best foundations in the Classics for any student, and it gives a learning-different student a real edge when they enter college. Visit www.angelicumacademy.com for more information.

The Seton Home School Curriculum

In his Letter to Families, Pope John Paul II wrote: "Parents are the first and the most important educators of their own children, and they also possess a fundamental competence in this area; they are educators because they are parents."

This quotation from His Holiness sums up very well the philosophy of Seton Home Study School, which is particularly tailored to Catholic families. They assist parents by providing counseling by phone, message boards, fax and email, as well as daily lesson plans, testing services, books, software, videos, and other educational materials. Seton serves an enrollment of approximately 10,000 homeschool students, and several thousand more families through book sales and by furnishing materials to small Catholic schools.

This curriculum is rigorous as well, but if you have a high-functioning learning-different child, it may be a good choice. The focus is development of written skills needed for a successful college career. Visit www.setonhome.org for more information.

Kolbe Academy Home School

Kolbe offers academic advising to assist is setting and meeting goals; quarterly inspection of work and examinations; detailed feedback at any time; access to Latin, Greek, math and science experts; and comprehensive record-keeping, including official transcripts and letters of recommendation.

School of Tomorrow (Lighthouse Academy, Lewisville, Texas)

Their curriculum is broken into 50-page increments. The students must complete 10 to 12 pages at a time and then take a test on the material, and they must achieve 80 percent or better on the material to move on. If they do not attain this grade, they must review the material and test again.

This curriculum is a win-win for the learning-different child; they will never have any grade less than an 80 percent on their transcripts! It may take them awhile to achieve this, but by mastering the subject content, they will always achieve excellent grades. The format is great due to the fact that they must see and hear the information for a longer period of time to absorb the information. Visit www.schooloftomorrow.com or www.ace.com for more information.

A Becka Book Curriculum

This is a proven and widely accepted program designed to provide an excellent Christian education for those who teach their child at home. The DVD program features the master teachers of Pensacola Christian Academy, who give complete instruction in kindergarten through grade 6 and in all core subjects for grades 7 to 12. In addition, the DVDs will help you teach specialized subjects such as biology, algebra and Spanish. Visit www.abeka.org for more information.

* * *

The homeschool option is very exciting. The opportunities are endless, but you must discipline yourself to follow through with the proper record-keeping, and both parents must be on the same page about the entire process. This must be a team effort. One parent cannot carry the whole load. Make sure that God is in the center of your decision, and this may turn out to be the best decision you have ever made.

PRIVATE THERAPISTS

Private therapists can be a godsend to a family, but they can also be a detriment if they are not properly certified. If a therapist is trained in one or more remedial language programs whose courses are IMSLEC-certified and they have been certified as a Certified Academic Language Therapist (C.A.L.T.), then you know you are getting a quality individual who will guide your child through the proper processes. Below is information about IMSLEC certification taken from their website (www.im slec.org). This shows you how in-depth a therapist's education must be in the field of learning differences:

> The International Multisensory Structured Language Education Council (IMSLEC), a 501(c)(3) organization, accredits quality Multisensory Structured Language Education (MSLE) training courses. Accredited courses, which meet IMSLEC criteria and instructional program standards for preparing specialists in Multisensory Structured Language Education. IMSLEC accredits training programs, which include a variety of approaches such as Orton-Gillingham, SEE (Sequential English Education) Spalding, Hardman, Alphabetic Phonics, Slingerland, and Alphabetic Phonetic Structural Linguistics. These training programs offer extensive coursework and supervised teaching experience leading to professional certification. The training programs may be independent post-secondary training programs or may exist within already accredited institutions, such as colleges, universities or medical entities.

> IMSLEC promotes and ensures quality Multisensory Structured Language Education (MSLE) training for teachers and therapists of individuals with dyslexia and related disorders through accreditation of training courses.

MSLE instruction includes the approaches, which incorporate components demonstrated to assist individuals with dyslexia and related disorders to gain literacy skills.

You can also visit the Academic Language Therapists Association website (www.altaread.org) to find Certified Academic Language Therapists (C.A.L.T.) in your area, and to find out more about certification.

* * *

Whatever option or combination of options you choose for your child's education, remember how important it is for everyone involved to see him or her for who he or she is: a wonderful, uniquely gifted image-bearer of God who is full of promise, potential and possibility. And with the right education, your child will believe it, too!

9

Higher Education:
Will They Make It?

A cheerful heart is good medicine, but a crushed spirit dries up the bones.
PROVERBS 17:21

Learning-different children have a unique perspective on the world. Most of them see the world as a beautiful and good place, but when they try to interact with it there seems to be an invisible barrier that won't let them pass. Their perceptions of others and the fairness of things is a little bit clouded. Their struggle with poor auditory processing can create a world that sounds muffled and hard to fully understand. We parents, often times, try to pull our children along through that invisible barrier and expect them to function well in all situations. But when it comes to your child's future, pulling her along can lead to frustration and disappointment. This is the time to stand next to her and look through that invisible barrier. See what she sees and how she sees it. Understanding how she perceives her world will give you insight for how to guide her toward a healthy and prosperous future.

As the elementary and middle school years come to a close, many parents feel that the worst is behind them; they are now experts on dealing with learning differences. They have safely crossed the Sea of Denial with their family intact. But the truth is, these early years have been preparation for the greatest challenge: high school and beyond. The good news is that if parents place themselves in God's hands, continuing to trust the One who brought them this far, He will continue to guide them through whatever lies ahead.

I like to recommend the following formula: Be a parent to your child from ages 0–10; guide them through life from ages 10–20; be their friend from age 20 until death. Your child will welcome your friendship and wise input in their adult years as you guide them through their adolescence. This process starts by setting them up to win in high school.

The majority of learning-different children make it through high school because their parents stay on top of the issues related to learning differences. Others have a more difficult time. To help your child through his struggles, start by listening to him. What are his dreams and goals? Though some of these may seem out of reach, treat all goals the same: with respect, joy and excitement. Your teen will pick up on your belief in him and believe that he might just make something of himself. Many learning-different kids have the ability to visualize the big picture. This is a strength. Their difficulty is trying to implement it. Because that is the case, the next step is to show your teen how to begin to make his dreams a reality.

> As Christian parents, we must instill in our children an unshakeable belief that God doesn't make mistakes.

Goals are the foundation of most everything we accomplish as human beings. They give us a direction and set us on a course to fulfill our potential. Without them, we wander aimlessly through life, wondering why our lives never amounted to anything. God wants great things for us. He provides opportunities for us to succeed, but all too often we don't believe that we have what it takes to make our dreams come true. Too many times, we ignore God's opportunities and settle for the status quo. As Christian parents, we must instill in our children an unshakeable belief that God doesn't make mistakes, and that He *expects* us to live up to our potential.

Start by asking your teen what she thinks she might like to do for a living. Make a list with her of all of her choices. Often young adults say, "I don't know." Don't worry; keep sharing with her the strengths you see in her. Challenge her to dream big as she imagines her future, and her reluctance (which is likely rooted in fear) will eventually melt away.

Now that you have the big picture, work backward to figure out the steps your teen needs to take to reach her big-picture goal. Create one-week goals, one-month goals, and six-month goals. These goals should be doable. Do not make them so difficult that they are impossible to achieve.

As I mentioned, my learning-different daughter Jackie has a real talent in music. She can sing like nobody's business and she can write song lyrics in her sleep. (She had published poetry by the time she finished her eighth-grade year.) Jackie told us that she really wanted to do music for her life's work. At the same time, Chris, our older son, was attending a local Catholic high school and was very active in the school band. He told us that he wanted to be the head of worldwide marketing for a major computer company.

Instead of blowing them off as if their dreams were ridiculous, we decided to take their dreams seriously. To do so, we worked backward from their big-picture goals. We looked at each individual dream and asked what we had to do today to make sure Chris and Jackie reached their goals tomorrow. We laid out the steps that had to be taken in order for them

to get there. Ultimately, Chris and Jackie had to make the final choice: Would they take the steps necessary to make their dreams come true? Giving them the power to decide empowered them to take ownership of their lives and their futures.

Jackie had the good fortune to record her own album and to use her music for God in many venues. As she experienced the fruits of her careful and determined plan, she eventually decided to change her course. She is currently finishing a college major in communications for film and TV, with a dream (and a plan) to pursue a career in television.

Chris took the steps toward his goals throughout his high school career by working for a local computer retail store. He laid the foundation of his work ethic and carries that with him to this day. He is now working in the worldwide marketing department for that prominent computer company.

For both Chris and Jackie, homeschooling was the right choice for them to get their high school education. They were best able to implement their plans and work toward their goals in that environment. My other two children are currently in high school and college, and neither of them would have done well in a homeschool situation. The right choice for realizing their dreams is an education at the Shelton School and Loyola Marymount University.

Our second son, Nick, dreams of making his mark in international business. Obviously, being multilingual will be important to his success. Becoming fluent in multiple languages is difficult for most people, but for learning-different students, it poses particular challenges. Nick knows that he must succeed in this area, and he also knows how he learns best. He has begun to learn Italian by listening to lessons on his iPod. Whenever he is not working, he listens on his headphones, trying to become fluent. He is taking the steps, one by one, that lie between him and his dreams.

Our youngest, Alicia, is a junior in high school, and we are working backward with her to make her big-picture dreams of a career in journalism and design become a reality.

Each child had different dreams and motivations, and every family comes with varied and special dynamics. Because of these factors, there is no "one size fits all" approach to your child's future. The one question that can be answered is, "Have other children with similar differences succeeded in college and beyond?" Yes! Some have chosen college, with all of its challenges, while others have chosen to go to trade school. Either way, many experience successful careers and deeply fulfilled lives. So much depends on the family's willingness to move on and guide their child to a world of adventure and happiness.

COLLEGE OR UNIVERSITY

Here is an example of working backward if your child's goals involve attending college or university:

	Weekly goal	Monthly goal	Six-month goal	Yearly goal
School	Do assignments as soon as I get them. Review my notes from class for 45 minutes every day.	Find a good group of people to create a study group. Let the professor know how I test best. Make sure that I use all of the accommodations available to me.	Pass my first semester classes with a B average or better. Look into some outside activity to meet people on campus.	Make some new friends. Pass my first year with good grades.
Work	Work five hours a week and see how that works with my studies.	Save one-third of what I make to help pay tuition.	If I am doing well, and can handle more hours, do so.	Add up the total I have contributed toward college. Evaluate what more I can do next year.
God	Pray for half an hour daily.	Find out what Christian activities are available on campus. Participate in at least one of them.	Evaluate participation in that activity and make any needed changes.	Try to increase the amount of time I spend in prayer.

Depending on the student, it may be a good idea to attend the local junior college for one or two years. Often, learning-different students make a smoother transition from high school to college if they are near home for a period of time. They need their family support system to guide them in understanding how college works. Remember, many in this population are emotionally behind about two years from their peers, so given the pressures of college life, it is not a bad idea to keep them close to home those first two years. If you have a child who is more independent and understands how to be his own advocate for his learning difference, then he may transition into a four-year university with no problem. Talk with your teen, his teachers and youth leaders to determine which environment will be best for him.

Research the college and university options available to students with learning differences. Peterson's *Colleges with Programs for Students with Learning Disabilities or ADD* is a great help when you are first getting started (a new edition is published every year). This catalog shows everything a parent needs to know to help your child choose the right university or college. Most colleges and universities in the country have outstanding programs available to learning-different students. The only "catch" is that students must learn how to be their own best advocate. The university will not hunt the student down to make sure that everything is running correctly, but they are available when the student comes looking for help.

When evaluating your choices, a key is student-teacher ratio. Most learning-different students get the one-on-one attention they need at a ratio of no more than 15:1.

Most colleges and universities want to have current testing, done within the last three years. In that testing they will be looking for the specific difficulties the student faces and what accommodations need to be made. Set up a time to meet with the college's learning-different specialist to determine how the accommodations will be implemented.

> **Most colleges and universities in the country have outstanding programs available to learning-different students.**

Many universities provide a note-taker to students with learning differences. The note-taker compiles detailed notes of your student's class sessions, puts them into an envelope and delivers them to your student's school mailbox. No one in the class knows who the notes are for, which keeps your student's learning style confidential. (Your student will still be required to attend all lectures and class sessions; the notes are to supplement what he or she is learning in the classroom.)

Because learning-different students have great difficulty reading and comprehending large quantities of material, audio textbooks are often available as well. (There is a great tool called the ClassMate Reader that helps students with dyslexia to read large quantities of text more easily. Check out the website at www.humanware.com and click on the link for learning disabilities. A short video will give you the information.)

These are just two of the accommodations available to the learning-different student at most colleges and universities. All too often, the main reason for failure in the college or university system is not the institution but the student. They have lived so long with parents and teachers telling them what to do and when that they do not yet know how to be successful unless they do everything they are told. They are desperate to prove to the world that they can succeed on their own, and often don't seek the help they need. In my experience, this denial can last anywhere from six months to a year, which is a burden on parents footing the tuition bill. If you are not sure that your child is ready to take responsibility for his or her learning difference and get the help he or she needs in university, look again at the junior college option. A time of transition may be just what he or she (and your pocketbook) needs.

It is imperative to teach your learning-different child how to be her own best advocate. This means, first, that she must understand her learning difference and accept it. (If we parents can't accept it, how can she?) Second, she must know how she learns best. Is she a visual learner? An auditory learner? Kinesthetic? She must know where to sit every time to get the most out of each class. Third, she must let the professor know about her learning difference and how she will best learn in the classroom. (Some professors will give tests according to a student's learning style. For example, they might give oral exams or multiple choice.) Some professors may be uninterested at first, but with gentle reminders they will watch the student's tenacity and come to appreciate their differences.

At one point, my son Nick thought he might want to go to medical school. He attended an inquiry session from a particular university on the West Coast. After the session, he went up to the university representative to introduce himself and said, "I am really looking forward to coming to the university. I'm looking into your medical school, but can you tell me what you have to offer the learning-different student? I am dyslexic." The gentleman was so taken aback at my son's cool and confident demeanor that he answered, "Certainly we will have all accommodations available to you. We certainly look forward to having you apply with us for the fall semester." Nick continues to be an advocate for his education.

Jackie, at first, believed she could do it on her own without any help. She attended junior college for two years, and her first year was a disaster. She was not her own best advocate, and it showed. Yet as she saw her choices steering her away from her goals, she decided to use the accommodations available to her. She is now completing her senior year in a university on the East Coast with a 3.9 GPA. She has received 90 percent of her tuition on an academic scholarship. She has succeeded because she knows how she learns best and is now unafraid to advocate on her own behalf.

TRADE SCHOOLS AND VOCATIONAL TRAINING

Your learning-different child may or may not choose college as his or her path to realizing his or her dreams. Another alternative may be trade school or a vocational training program. Depending on your child's abilities and interests, these options may be a perfect fit. Trade and vocational programs also typically take a shorter period of time to complete than college, which allows students to move toward a career sooner rather than later. Let's take a closer look at what this form of education is all about.

Unfortunately, vocational instruction has sometimes worn the stigma of a poor man's education. Yet prior to the twentieth century, vocational learning was simply referred to as an apprenticeship, and it was the primary mode of career training most people received. Individuals learned their trade by the side of local craftsmen, whether they were blacksmiths or merchants, or later, mechanics or welders.

As the twentieth century plowed forward, vocational and trade education diversified into other industries, including information technology, tourism, retail and manufacturing. Today, trade schools are advertised on television throughout the day, and some of the bad rap they've gotten is due to poor marketing and image strategies. In spite of this, vocational education is overcoming its image by giving individuals diverse opportunities to create a bright future.

As I researched this topic, I was pleased to find that stringent accreditation criteria are in place for several programs to ensure high-quality, expert instruction and on-the-job training. There are a number of trade schools, online schools, technical schools and community colleges that are accredited to these rigorous standards.

Distance learning may be a good option for your learning-different child. As of this writing, there are more than 23 million students in the United States taking distance-learning courses. As this number has swelled over the past 5 to 10 years, accreditation has become more robust and stringent to ensure that students receive the best education available to them. (For more information about distance-learning programs, visit www.directoryofschools.com.)

Some of the online certification programs that might be good possibilities for learning-different students are:

- **DeVry University**—Areas of study include biomedical and health, business, networking, technology management, electronics, telecommunications, computer training and sales (www.devry.edu).

- **American InterContinental University**—Opportunities include healthcare, human resources, marketing, Internet security, instructional technology and digital design (www.aiuonline.edu).

- **The Art Institute of Pittsburgh**—Study graphic design, interior design, game art and design, Web design and interactive media, culinary management and residential planning (www.aionline.edu).

- **Capella University**—Certification in areas including human resource management, project management, addictions counseling, criminal justice and marriage and family services (www.capella.edu).

- **ITT Technical Institute**—Learn Web design, IS administration, business accounting, computer forensics or criminal justice (www.itt-tech.edu).

- **University of Phoenix**—Earn certification in project management, technology management, health care education, school nursing, IS security or visual communication (www.phoenix.edu).

Many of these programs are a hybrid of vocational training and a university-level education. The great news for learning-different students is that they can take their time completing their coursework. (This can also be a big plus if the student needs to work while receiving his or her education.)

Maybe distance learning is not for your child; perhaps working with her hands is what God is calling her to do. If that is the case, opt for an accredited skilled trade school with a good reputation for job placement. Various trade schools offer certification for automotive repair persons, heating and air conditioning servicepersons, electricians, aircraft and transportation dispatchers, aviation maintenance persons, power generation technicians, power plant operators, wind power technicians and emergency medical technicians (EMTs). These careers are often well-paying and in high demand. Visit www.educationcenteronline.org and click on "Trade Schools" for more information.

Whether you and your teen decide that college, vocational training or trade school is the best option for him, setting reachable short- and long-term goals is the key to success. Goal-keeping will help your child achieve his full potential according to God's plan. Lay out the tools before him and show him how to use those tools, and the world will be his.

SECTION FOUR

AT HOME WITH YOUR LEARNING-DIFFERENT CHILD

10

Marriage Matters

Often when a couple gets a diagnosis of learning difference for their child, it is the mother who receives the information. She is usually the first one to notice that the child's behavior is off from other children. She is often the first one to receive the test results from a professional; the husband is at work and hears the diagnosis from her perspective.

Let's face it, ladies: When we get a piece of unsettling news, we want to talk it over with someone. If our husband is not available, we call Mom or our girlfriends. Having a support system is good, but it's very easy to let everyone else's opinion on the subject become our foundation for the "learning-different truth." Then, when our husband comes home, we immediately download the information (in its entirety) from the professional, filtered through our mother and girlfriends. Husbands know what we've been up to. They know the information should be taken with a grain of salt; it can't be as bad as we are making it out to be. His reaction looks something like this: "Oh, Johnny will be fine. So he reads a little slow . . . he'll pick it up. He's just lazy. We just have to come down on him a little harder. What else happened in your day?" Instead of drawing together as a team to protect and nurture our family wisely, we are already at odds.

What is funny is that we women have a tendency to accept this state of affairs, playing our role as a tightrope walker with pride. We see ourselves as the head lioness, protecting both her lion cub and her mate. We want to give Johnny everything he needs to succeed, but maybe our husband is right (even though he doesn't understand too much about learning differences) and we shouldn't get too uptight.

We walk the tightrope, and all the while, Johnny is still having a difficult time at school and at home with his siblings. Instead of getting him the help he desperately needs, we do endless research to feel in control of the situation. (I can't tell you how many mothers come into my office armed with the latest "cure" for their child, yet who are unwilling to commit to the therapies recommended for him.) The tension continues to mount on the family and the marriage.

This dance sets couples up for a stressful marriage. God saw in the two of you the possibility of two special people working as a team to raise His special creation, your child. He never proposed that you work against each other . . . which is exactly what is happening in the scenario above.

The frustration level for both the husband and the wife can spin out of control unless the couple surrenders their weakness of pride to God. He can bring balance back into any marriage. We are all human and we may have to surrender our prideful nature a thousand times a day. And each time we do, our marriage will become stronger.

Then he took the book of the covenant, and read it in the hearing of the people; and they said, "All that the

LORD has spoken we will do, and we will be obedient" (Exod. 24:7).

But he said to me, "My grace is sufficient for you, for my power is made perfect in weakness." Therefore I will boast all the more gladly about my weaknesses, so that Christ's power may rest on me (2 Cor. 12:9).

But this precious treasure—this light and power that now shines within us—is held in perishable containers, that is, in our weak bodies. So everyone can see that our glorious power is from God and is not our own (2 Cor. 4:7).

When pride comes, then comes disgrace; but with the humble is wisdom (Prov. 11:2).

Remember that because learning differences are hereditary, it's likely that one or both of you is dealing with it yourself. It's also likely that your learning difference is affecting your marriage. I have worked with many adults with AD/HD, and communication in marriage is one of the main difficulties they face. The spouse who does not have the learning difference (or whose learning difference is less severe) often feels that the other does not listen to him or her. If the relationship is not handled with maturity and grace (on both spouses' parts), one of two things is likely to happen: The non-learning-different spouse handles every aspect of family life (including finances, child discipline, planning and scheduling, and so on) or he or she leaves the marriage. The high divorce rate among families with learning differences reflects the difficulty many couples have solving their marital problems. As Colleen Alexander-Roberts writes:

Marriages can be pushed to the limit. It is not difficult to understand how marital problems can grow in a family system that has not been functioning in a normal manner. (This is not to imply that all families with a child with AD/HD are dysfunctional, because that is not the case.) When the child with AD/HD reaches adolescence many parents are burned out and frustrated as a result of things such as fighting the school system, nightly arguments over homework, handling the daily challenges of AD/HD, monitoring medications, etc. Parents who have advocated for years for their child may feel a tremendous sense of failure and loss of control as the teenage years emerge, and they find that things are not better or easier as they thought they would be. Social activities may have been limited through the years, so parents may no longer have close friends to lean on for support. In addition, parents may have become so entangled in the difficulties their child has experienced that they have neglected each other's needs and their marital relationship. Marital therapy may be necessary. We cannot underestimate the need for parents to spend quality time together despite the limitations they face.[1]

THE BLAKE FAMILY

The Blake family had two children, a boy and a girl. Their son was diagnosed with dyslexia and was attending an excellent learning-different school in their area. Tom Blake, the dad, owned his own business and appeared to be very successful, but he believed that he had a learning difference. He decided to get remediation for his poor reading skills, and hired me to help. I asked him why he wanted to proceed when he had already done so well for himself, having attended a great university and graduated at the top of his class. He said, "I cheated my way through college."

Tom had finally surrendered his pride and was getting on with reality: He was a poor reader and he wanted to change that. As the therapy progressed, he asked if his wife could come in to observe. He

> **Random Polls**
> Where do you most often get personal support for dealing with your child's struggles?
>
> 35% Spouse or partner
> 14% Extended family
> 20% Close friend or friends
> 5% Other parents or a support group
> 13% A therapist or counselor

said, "She doesn't understand why I'm doing this." Sandy came in and observed several times. As the three of us talked together, it became obvious to me that there were other difficulties within their marriage.

Most Saturdays, Sandy had a "honey-do" list for Tom to complete. She would tell him what she needed done, but he rarely did it; she usually had to complete it herself. Her perception was that Tom never listened to her and that they were drifting apart. In reality, Tom had auditory processing problems; he truly did not hear what Sandy was trying so hard to say to him.

Sandy and Tom are now using new techniques to work around his poor auditory processing skills. Sandy writes her "honey-do" list and posts it on the refrigerator. When she wants Tom to understand what she is saying, she makes sure that she looks at him in the eye and expresses herself well. Tom, in return, makes a habit of reflecting back to Sandy what he just heard her say. In addition, they have decided together to talk for 30 minutes each day in a quiet environment—no kids, no music, no TV. As Tom and Sandy have begun to deal with Tom's learning differences, they are both becoming more able to deal with their children's needs.

LET GOD USE IT!

It may be hard to believe, but God can use your learning differences to strengthen your marriage and your family. The very characteristics that make living with a learning difference easier—humor, humility and grace, to name just three—are the same traits that make a marriage happy and lasting. And the opposite is true, too: Your strong and healthy marriage can only help as you, your spouse and your family deal with the potential difficulties brought by learning differences. Let God use both to draw you together! (In the Resources section of this book, there is a five-week Bible study for married couples. I encourage you to complete it together, inviting the Lord to work in your marriage and in your family's learning differences for His glory.)

Families are incredibly resilient when God is at the center of them. Remember the old saying, "A family that prays together, stays together"? Well, it's true. When a family makes time every day to talk with God and with each other, and then asks God to guide them as they move forward together, the fruits of that family are bound to be plentiful. Children, learning-different or not, benefit from seeing their parents go to the Lord for guidance. Every day is a great opportunity to show your children how to deal with the stresses of life.

Let my prayer be counted as incense before thee, and
the lifting up of my hands as an evening sacrifice (Ps.
141:2, *KJV*).

11

Brothers and Sisters: Where Do I Fit In?

Sibling rivalry has been around since Cain and Abel, and it is part of the human condition. If you had brothers and sisters, think back to your own childhood. I bet you have several memories that bring a smile to your face.

My children sit around the dinner table and recall various antics they pulled to get each other in trouble. Through these tangled tales, I have discovered that I, at one time or another, treated each of them unjustly. As the truth has emerged, I have asked forgiveness for not picking up on these rivalries quickly enough. Trouble between siblings can be an opportunity for children to grow and mature, but sometimes, as in the story of Cain and Abel, sibling rivalry can go seriously wrong.

Siblings of learning-different children have another layer of difficulty to negotiate. Nearly all parents are unaware of the stress and confusion they must endure, swirling in the Sea of Denial all by themselves, trying to maneuver the currents to connect with their parents. They often feel ignored or neglected, and some will do almost anything to get their parents' attention. Some lash out physically. They may start fights with their learning-different sibling and then blame their brother or sister for the disagreement, eventually leading to tension and chaos in their relationship.

On the other hand, some children with a learning-different sibling may try very hard to be "the good child." They do whatever Mom and Dad say to keep the peace. They perceive very clearly that there is something wrong within the family, and by being good, they feel that they might fix it. Then Mom and Dad will be proud. This type of child holds their feelings in; the parents have no idea that their resentment runs deep.

Throughout my years as a language therapist, I have met several of these "good children." I have found that they have a very hard time being at school with their learning-different sibling. They make excuses to their peers for their sibling's behavior and distance themselves from their brother or sister to be accepted. They rarely share their dilemma at home, and because the learning-different child is unaware of their sibling's frustration, he or she continues the overbearing behavior.

Family and social life can be lonely for the non-learning-different sibling. But parents can help by balancing their time among the siblings. Try not to constantly "save" the learning-different child from every situation while the sibling drowns in his or her world of family confusion. Look for ways to spend time individually with each sibling, and allow each child to vent their feelings of frustration or anxiety. You may be surprised to learn that an older child is as worried about your child's learning difference as you are. Help your older child understand ways that he can help; if he learns more about his younger sibling's learning style, he may be better equipped to offer help with homework.

Younger siblings, on the other hand, rarely perceive the child with learning differences as being disabled. She is more likely to accept her older sibling at face value, and to be fully aware of his many strengths. After all, her older sibling has always been bigger, stronger and quite capable in many ways.

However, the younger child is less apt to understand why so much attention is focused on the sibling with AD/HD, dyslexia or another learning difference.

At some point, a younger sibling is likely to develop better reading and writing skills than the child with dyslexia. This can be a source

Random Polls
How understanding are family and close friends about your child's learning difficulties?

16% Very understanding
29% Somewhat under-standing
21% Not very understanding
31% Depends on the person

of confusion and resentment; the older child may feel embarrassed, and the younger child may not understand why her older brother needs extra help with skills she has easily mastered. It is important during this time that you answer the younger child's questions about learning differences. Explain that it is a learning difference, not an illness. Many children mistakenly believe that their sibling has some sort of disease.[1]

If parents are not wise enough to help non-learning-different siblings early on, anger and resentment may become their foundation for sibling relationships. Put yourself in their shoes. What if, every day, your parents only talked about your brother or sister? What if you felt pressured to make sure that your brother or sister did okay at school? "Just make sure Johnny fits in on the playground." The problem is, you realize Johnny doesn't know how to behave toward anyone on the playground and you know he won't listen to you. If this was your constant experience, you might wish that your learning-different sibling would just go away. Or you might decide to be "worse" to get the attention you want and need.

It is up to you to ensure that all your children are in the lifeboat as you maneuver through the Sea of Denial. The family will be strengthened, for the better, if everyone goes through the journey together.

TIPS FOR SIBLINGS

• Don't be afraid to talk to Mom and Dad if you feel they are spending too much time with your brother or sister. If you need more of them, let them know!

• Ask Mom and Dad for a special day that is just for you. You are just as important to Mom and Dad as your brother or sister.

• Talk about your frustrations and confusion with your parents. They won't be angry.

• Laugh! Don't take life too seriously.

Grandparent Input:
Bridging the Generations

Grandparents can be a child's greatest gift. Their wisdom can open the door to a child's imagination (not to mention that every visit, they have a surprise or two in store!). Grandchildren are a joy in old age, helping their grandparents to stay young. It's a relationship that can offer incredible benefits for both generations.

However, sometimes when a child is diagnosed with a learning difference, grandparents get caught in the "accuse the parent" current on the Sea of Denial. Their lack of education on the subject can damage the relationship between the parents and the grandparents. It is difficult for grandparents to be the support that is needed if they refuse to educate themselves. If grandparents want to stay connected to the family, they must educate themselves as much as the parents about learning differences.

Learning-different children need structure and specific rules to live successfully. Yet often when children visit Grandma and Grandpa, structure and rules go out the window. Unfortunately, instead of owning up to the part they have played, grandparents sometimes assume that when a child acts out, his or her parents must be doing something wrong. Grandparents may feel the need to give parenting advice, not knowing that traditional parenting is not effective with learning-different kids.

Other times, grandparents feel sorry for their grandchild's predicament and get caught in the sympathy current on the Sea of Denial. Generally, children do not like to be pitied, and this is even truer with learning-different children. A grandparent's persistent sympathy can destroy family relationships. Remember, sympathy lowers the bar of potential for the child, but empathy forces you to put a plan into action.

Random Polls
How much time per year do you get for a complete break from parenting?

- 5% Two weeks or more
- 15% 4 to 7 days
- 11% 3 days or fewer
- 63% Just a few hours here and there
- 3% Other

As an empathetic grandparent, you can help your children parent this unique child, helping your grandchild become who God intended him or her to be. Get out of the "accuse the parent" and sympathy currents and move into the lifeboat of communication, education and empathy.

Once you are safely aboard, ask your children how you can carry over their parenting skills into your home to create consistency in the child's life. Offer to take the children on occasion to give them a break now and again. Raising a learning-different child can be exhausting and sometimes overwhelming because the demands are much greater.

You can be an incredible support for your family as they navigate this journey together. Don't be afraid of this task; God will guide you.

Here are some great tips for when the grandkids come for a few days.

GRANDPARENTING TIPS FOR GRANDKIDS WITH LEARNING DIFFERENCES

- When the children arrive, sit them down and share the house rules. (Make sure that these are the same or similar to those at their home.)

- Keep your voice calm and low. Remember, yelling is not an option! All it does is stimulate the brain for more chaos.

- Give one direction at a time and make sure your grandchild has understood what you are saying. Have him repeat back to you what you just said.

- Bend down to her level and make eye contact for clear communication.

- Touch his arm slightly to make sure that he is aware that you need his attention.

- If the child makes a scene or misbehaves, make sure that you have a timeout area where she must stay. There must not be any entertainment available to her in this location.

- Keep her in the timeout area a minute for every year of her life. (If she is five years old, she must stay there five minutes.)

· Learning-different children need as much physical exercise as possible. Make sure that you plan that into your time with them.

· Take the time to enjoy the simple things with your grandkids.

· Love them and spoil them, but most of all, *be consistent*.

Moving Forward Together

When a mother first hears the words "You are pregnant," the mystery of life begins to unfold in all its glory. When you feel life move inside of you, there is no greater joy in all the world, and the love for your child grows with each passing day. You cannot believe that anyone could love this child more than you do.

In reality, God does love your child more than you ever could. He allows you to care for His creation for a short time. He entrusts His treasure to you, but He wants to be included in the raising of this child. He understands your disappointment about the differences of your child, but He wants to draw you closer to Himself through this experience. You have an opportunity to understand true joy and love through this experience. He is waiting for you to accept it, so paddle through the Sea of Denial knowing He is on the other side to catch you in His arms.

LET'S REVIEW

Don't forget the Edison gene, which is important for the survival of humankind. Without that gene, who will take risks to push humanity forward in thinking, physical challenges or even finding new worlds?

Understand your child's diagnosis. Don't be afraid of it; embrace it. Draw close to God to find out why He has chosen you to parent your child and how He wants you to do it.

If your child's behavior is off a bit from his peers, don't ignore it; explore it. Find out where and how he is off and get to a professional to help you understand what is happening. Don't think you know it all; you don't. Ask for help.

Stay positive in your discipline, Mom and Dad. Consistency, consistency, consistency, consistency is the key to great parenting.

Educate yourself about your child's education. Don't be afraid to explore all the educational options available to her. Don't forget private therapists and all they have to offer.

When looking toward your child's future, don't be afraid to raise the bar and give him opportunities for his dreams to become a reality. Remember, these dreams belong to him, not to you. Look at the end goal and ask yourself, "What can I do today to make my child's dream become a reality tomorrow?"

Is college or trade school for your child? Work out what each option looks like. Pick the avenue that best suits her and her goals. The most important thing to remember is to encourage her in whatever direction she chooses.

Marriage is a sacrament and should be treated with respect. When our married life is healthy, our children are healthy mentally, spiritually and physically. If your marriage is going through a hard time, address it now.

Stay connected with all members of the family. Siblings need separate time away with each parent. Make special dates with each child on a regular basis. Grandparents want and need to be a part of the family. Educate them about learning differences and how they can play a role in the lives of their learning-different grandchild.

How do you help your child best? Pray, pray, pray. Ask God to help you every step of the way. He will not let you down. Just as your child trusts you to do the best for him, so we must trust God to help us through whatever lies ahead.

You have the tools you need to go through the Sea of Denial in peace and confidence, knowing that God will guide you every step of the way. Go forward and don't be afraid to change the world for the better through your child's learning difference.

RESOURCES

Don't Just Take It from Me: My Kids' Experiences in Their Own Words

I thought you might like to hear from my children's perspectives about what it feels like to have a learning difference and about what it's like growing up in a family where learning differences are part of everyday life. I asked each of them to write from their hearts, with no word limit. Here are their stories.

CHRIS

I was 10 when my mom first told me that my sister had something called ADD and that they were giving her some special medication to help her concentrate. At the time, I had no idea why anyone would need to take medication in order to concentrate. Looking back over the years, the most difficult thing for me was not being able to understand what my siblings were going through.

I watched them struggle through simple tasks like taking a pop quiz or sitting down to do their homework, and I couldn't understand why it was such a challenge for them. I couldn't understand why my mom needed to help my sister with her homework every night or why they were given extra time to take tests.

In junior high, my sister was sent to a school that catered specifically to children with ADD. It was very interesting. I noticed an immediate change—she seemed happy again, something

I hadn't seen in quite some time. However, I couldn't understand why someone would need to go to a school that catered to learning-different children. What was so special about it? To me, it just seemed like an expensive school where you were given as long as you needed to take a test and where the coursework was easier.

I was one year ahead of my sister when she started high school. I thought because she went to this special school throughout junior high that she was "cured" and that things would be back to normal when she started high school. But the majority of my fellow students suffered from the same ignorance as I did; they couldn't understand why she didn't fit in with everyone else. My sister's first year of high school was probably the most difficult thing I've ever seen anyone go through. The teachers had no idea how to present the material in a way that she could understand it, and I constantly had to wait for her after school so that she could finish detention. It was a difficult time.

She got through it and has since graduated college. When I saw her receive her diploma, I was so proud! I think about how much of a challenge school was for me and I can't begin to imagine seeing it through her eyes. We grew up in a time when ADD was such a new thing and there were several misconceptions about how to deal with it.

Although I will never fully be able to comprehend the scope of what it means to grow up suffering from ADD, having watched my siblings go through it, I now have a better understanding. I only wish that I would have had the knowledge I have today so that I would have been able to better support them through those rough times.

But you live and you learn, and because of those past experiences, I now have a better understanding of what it means to be learning-different. And if someday my own children have a learning disability, I feel better equipped to give them the resources they need in order to be successful.

JACKIE

ADD has had many faces throughout my life. As I have gone through life's various transitions and phases, I have been able to witness my ADD growing and changing with me. From my earliest memory until now I have always felt different, but I didn't realize it until recently.

From very early on, I can remember not being able to get comfortable when trying to fall asleep. My mind raced nonstop. This went on for many years, even into my early teens (but I wouldn't dare tell anybody). When I was around five, I began to develop phobias. I always thought I might throw up, even if I was fine. My parents reassured me countless times, but I needed to keep hearing that I was going to be okay.

I found it much easier to make friends, learn and interact in early primary school than I did later in life. I just felt like an average kid. I would draw, play, sing and learn to read and write. I have many wonderful memories.

By the time I was in fifth grade, however, most of my experiences were negative. I believe that this is the point in my life when my ADD took over (as I'd like to put it). The process of discovering that I learn and remember things differently than other people was incredibly painful. I had difficulty with the spelling words, math problems and history questions. They all required memorization. I didn't understand or retain anything that was being taught, and I didn't know why. At home, my mom would stay up with me until midnight most nights helping me with homework and getting me through my tantrums. I'd get frustrated, then she'd get frustrated and then I would cry myself to sleep.

In sixth grade, my parents took me to get tested for ADD, and I began taking medication shortly after that. After the first week, I finally felt, in some sense, "normal." I was able to retain and repeat things, which had really never happened to me before. I honestly believe that my life would have been more difficult and completely different had I never gone on my medication. Frankly, it meant that I could finally open doors on my own, doors that might have remained closed to me.

In seventh and eight grades, my problems shifted from schoolwork to relationships and interactions with others. Of course, I wanted to fit in and be accepted, but I was not (in my mind) like everyone else. I found it very difficult to relate and communicate with others. I said and did things without thinking, and in most cases it came out all wrong and inevitably someone was upset with me. I didn't feel like I was in control of myself; I felt like I was watching myself say and do things, but couldn't control my own actions. As my social life worsened into ninth grade, I began to give up on myself. I felt like something was really different and wrong with me. The only bright spot was using my music to express how I felt. I wrote lyrics and tried to perfect my vocal sound. I started receiving job offers to perform.

When my parents approached me about homeschooling, I jumped at the chance. Now I would have the chance to focus on my music. I was done with all of the other school drama.

Over the next three years, my mother taught me my daily lessons. She was patient and understood what I needed. She seemed to instinctively know how to teach me with my particular learning difference. She taught me in a way that I could succeed.

After graduating high school, I was burned out on studying. I didn't know how I was going to make it to college, and decided to take a year off to just breathe. I worked most of the time and music was the rest of my life. That year off was something I needed, and I used the time to make friends and discover life on my terms rather than on everyone else's. When the year was up, I felt the urge to give college a try. Through a lot of hard work and determination, I made it into college with scholarships.

My college experience wasn't a typical one. I was older than most freshmen coming in and I was determined to work hard. I learned everything on note cards. I recited things over and over again, even in the shower or while eating dinner. When it came time for tests, I finally understood what *studying* really meant. For the first time, I knew what it felt like to ace a test. Not until college did I get to experience that, and it was that much sweeter because I did it all on my own. I managed to pass all my classes by using tools I had learned along the way to help with my ADD. I learned how to communicate and to develop friendships, and finally began feeling like I was exactly where I was supposed to be.

This past May I graduated from college, and when I was walking across the stage to receive my diploma, I could swear time slowed down. That day, I had my family and closest friends there to support me. I felt untouchable. Many said I couldn't finish college, and to them I say, "Thank you." Many hurt me and few cared, and to them I say, "Thank you." I finally see that everything I was given was exactly the way it was supposed to be.

ADD is not a curse but a blessing. It took me 23 years to realize that. I am very proud of all that I have accomplished, because I remember where I was and how hard I had to work to get where I am today. ADD has given me proof that there is no "normal." I am now who I was meant to be. The road from here is just another step in the discovery, and I am courageously going down that road every day.

NICK

The average student is expected to have a rigorous academic life and faces a number of major obstacles. Having a learning difference makes the academic experience that much more difficult, but I would not trade places with anyone else if I had the opportunity to get rid of the so-called "disability."

The first time my learning difference became noticeable in my life was when I was in the fourth grade. What was supposed to be a fun time became a terrible experience. I would get very nervous when I had to answer in class; I believed that I'd never get the answer right. I tried to distract the teacher by saying or doing things I thought were funny.

I also fidgeted with my pencil. Many times I fidgeted so much that I broke my pencil. I can't tell you how many times my name was put on the board for broken pencils. I've never understood this type of discipline and I never will. It is obvious to me now that the teacher did not know what to do with a learning-different kid.

As time went on, school became more challenging and I was constantly falling behind the other students in my basic lessons. I had to constantly struggle to stay focused and often dazed off into my own dreamland. When the teacher called on me I was completely lost, and I was picked on by the other students.

My lifesaver was when I was diagnosed with dyslexia and ADD. I know that when I say diagnosis was my lifesaver, most people cannot understand. Many might think that the world had ended, finding out that they or their own children were diagnosed with a disability. However, in the grand scheme of things, having dyslexia, ADD or any form of learning difference is not that big of a deal if you know how to treat it.

If it wasn't for my mother, I would have been completely lost. When she found out that I was suffering from these differences, she jumped into action and learned how to fix it. The lesson to all parents is not to be so stubborn or pretend that these problems don't exist. I can remember friends that shared the same learning differences as I did. Many of their parents were always whining about the fact that their kid wasn't "with it" enough or "like other kids" enough. I would have loved to say to them, "Can I get you some cheese with your whine?"

I was fortunate enough to attend a school that specialized in helping students with learning differences. For me, medicine wasn't necessary. However, I had to work harder than most in every aspect of my life. With the skills I was taught, I could not ask to be in a better position than I am now. After finishing high school, I attended two years of college at Loyola Marymount University in Los Angeles, California. Now I am finishing my last two years at a very prestigious school in Switzerland.

Without the support of everyone who has helped me on my journey, I would not have been able to get where I am today.

One thing that always pushed me forward when trouble faced me was to remember that some of the greatest minds in history suffered from learning differences—and they changed the world as we know it. I am in great company with people like Albert Einstein, Charles Schwab and Paul Orfalea, all of whom suffered from the challenges I face every day.

Anything is possible, no matter the circumstances. I urge anyone faced with a learning disability to get help. Don't attempt to take this journey alone. Remember: With support, great things are possible for anyone.

ALICIA

Ever since I can remember, it has been difficult for me to learn or to grasp certain concepts that others find simple. I've always known something caused me to learn differently.

Attending a private school as a child was probably the hardest experience for me as a learning-different student. The first time I recall being out of place occurred in my second-grade science class. We were going over the parts of the human body and were assigned to color and label the various body parts. I worked strenuously for over an hour, matching the different words to the appropriate parts.

When I finished, I walked over to my teacher's desk to hand my work in. "What is this?" she shrieked. She gave me a look of terror, and immediately ripped the paper into multiple pieces. I remember her throwing my paper into the trash bin in front of the entire classroom. I didn't see anything wrong with the work I had done, which made me believe there was something wrong with me.

As I entered the fourth grade, I began noticing my weak study habits and my constant obsession with making perfect grades. I had the tendency to procrastinate and would come to my mother the day before a test, begging her to review the material with me. If I missed a question, I wound up on the floor in tears, wondering how I could possibly miss such a simple word problem.

Another major factor through the years was my inability to listen. As my family sat around the dinner table discussing the highlights of their day, my mind would wander, listening in on only bits and pieces of the conversation. I tried to concentrate on listening, but I only comprehended half of what was being said. My family would get upset with me, thinking that I was just spacing out.

By the time I reached middle school, I was at the point of almost giving up. School days seemed like a blur. It was difficult for me to remember any of the material I learned. I began having severe migraines and my immune system seemed to be at an all-time low. I felt like I was seconds away from having a mental breakdown. While completing my homework one night, I remember crying hysterically to my parents about how frustrated I got when it came to school. They finally came to the conclusion that it was time for me to transfer to a public school. I was so relieved about the decision; I felt as though I could finally breathe.

The public school system was a godsend and a curse. I never had to apply myself to make As in my courses. Although this was great at the time, it didn't prepare me for high school in the least. At the same time, I spent a lot of time alone, not wanting to go out. I began to have irritable moods and slept most of the day away. I was soon diagnosed with depression.

My parents decided to send me to a new private high school, which I enjoyed when I first began. After being there for only a few short months, my outlook changed. The workload began to increase and my grades began to slip, making me feel as though I was in elementary school a second time. The kids in my grade seemed to understand the material, which made me believe I was unintelligent. Math was a constant struggle for me. The numbers in a problem always seemed to move around the board, making it nearly impossible to understand. I ended my freshman year with a mixture of Cs and Bs.

The first day of my sophomore year, I sat in the back of my history class listening to my teacher discuss the curriculum for the year. At that moment, I knew I couldn't be there a moment longer. My brother had recently graduated from Shelton, and I had seen firsthand how he had embraced his challenges. That night, while lying in bed, I had a revelation. I knew that if I continued to stay at my current school, my high school years would be total chaos. Therefore, I had a long talk with my parents about the future. We talked about what was happening with my learning and we discussed the successes Nick found at Shelton. After our conversation, I was soon tested for learning differences. When the results came back, they revealed that I had auditory processing disorder and ADD.

I was enrolled in The Shelton School and put on the proper medication. My grades quickly changed to As and high Bs, and

I was happy because I could understand the concepts being taught. I thank God for such a blessing in disguise. Without such a drastic change, I know I would never have been as successful as I am today. I wish I could go back to several of the teachers who believed I was moronic for learning differently. In a way, I'm thankful for my learning differences because I now understand I am able to take anything life throws at me.

* * *

Well, there you have it: learning differences from a child's perspective. I hope that their stories have brought insight and peace to you, and challenged you to embrace and even celebrate your child's learning differences.

Out of the Mouths of Babes: Quotes from Children with Learning Differences

What would you say to a friend who just found out
that he or she has a learning difference?

It's not the worst thing that could happen. You can still do great things! My life is better now than it was before. Now that my family and I know how my brain works I get the right help from the right people. Before I felt like I was the only one in the world who ever had a learning difference. Now I am happy because now I know that there are a lot of people who have them. (Benjamin, age 9)

When you first find out you get kind of scared because you think that they can't fix you. But when the people show you how to read better, you realize that you *can* do anything. (Jamie, age 8)

Don't be sad. Some more of us have it, too. (Taylor, age 6)

It's okay because now I can read better and no one makes fun of me. So you can read better too. And I will never make fun of you. (Jesse, age 7)

Before I found out I had a learning difference, I just thought I was stupid. Everyone else would always make really good grades and I never would. I would study more than all my friends and I never felt good enough. Then when I found out it was my learning difference, I realized I wasn't stupid . . . I just learn differently. Maybe you will see that you aren't stupid either. (Joey, age 13)

It is great to have a learning difference because you see things differently than everyone else. It is not always good to see everything the same. (Emily, age 10)

What do you want to be when you grow up?

I want to be an architect. (Benjamin, age 9)

I want to write books for children. I think that that would be fun. (Jamie, age 8)

I want to be a fireman or a policeman. (Taylor, age 6)

I want to be a doctor! (Jesse, age 7)

I haven't decided yet, but I know it will be great! (Joey, age 13)

I want to be an actress. (Emily, age 10)

How do you think your learning difference helps you?

It helps me because I can see things in 3D perspective. And that is pretty important when you are going to be an architect! (Benjamin, age 9)

It makes me notice more things in the world. I really like to watch animals and the things outside for a long time. When I watch them I get to see every little thing about them. But I don't understand why I get in trouble when I take so long to look at them. (Jamie, age 8)

I don't know. Maybe it makes me race around faster so I can get to where I want to go faster. (Taylor, age 6)

I think that it helps me because in math I see all the figures in my head clearly. Then it is easier for me to work the problem out. (Joey, age 13)

My learning difference makes me slow down to see things in a different way than other people. Sometimes I think this bothers people, but I like it because I see things in a new and better way. (Emily, age 10)

How do you and your family feel about your
learning difference?

We all understand it because all of us have it. It's really no big deal. (Benjamin, age 9)

I guess they like it. Sometimes I think that they [my parents] wish my learning difference were all better. (Jamie, age 8)

I don't know. All I know is that Mom and Dad fight a lot when they talk about it. I don't know what I did wrong. (Taylor, age 6)

No one in my family seems to care that I have it. They just hug me a lot. (Jesse, age 7)

My dad says that I am just lazy and that I should just try harder. My mom seems to understand. I am just glad that I am reading better. (Joey, age 13)

I think they like it. My mom works really hard since they found out I had a learning difference. (Emily, age 10)

Random Kid Quotes

The dream gods took my thoughts away and it is too hard to concentrate. So I don't think that I can do my work today. (First-grade student with AD/HD)

[Peeking through my office door] Can I learn to read in here? I really need some help. I can't read a thing. (First-grade student with dyslexia)

[When asked what she had just read] Words are floating in too many directions. (First-grade student with auditory processing disorder and dyslexia)

[Blurted out during a therapy session] Monsters come to your bed, you know, and eat your bad dreams. That's why I want to live in Australia. That is really true, you know. Do you need to go to Australia too? (First-grade student with dyslexia, ADD, auditory processing disorder)

I feel like a boulder was taken off of me now that I can read better. (Third-grade student with ADD)

I got a 100% on my spelling test today! Not bad for a dyslexic. (Third-grade student with dyslexia)

[After working on homework for more than three hours] I feel so old and wrinkled. I can't do anymore! (Seventh-grade student with dyslexia and ADD)

[Written] My tartly [turtle] can scud acros [across] the world cus [because] hes [he is] a supper [super] turtly [turtle]. (Third-grade student with ADD and dyslexia)

I had one idea, then I forgot it. Then I had another idea and I forgot that idea. But it is okay, because now I remember the first idea. (First-grade student with dyslexia and ADD)

Learning-Different
Schools in the United States

If you do not find a school in your area on the following list, you can contact the International Dyslexia Association at (410) 296-0232 for more information.

California
Charles Armstrong School
1405 Solona Drive
Belmont, CA 94002
(650) 592-7570
www.charlesarmstrong.org

The Prentice School
18341 Lassen Dr.
Santa Ana, CA 92705-2012
(714) 538-4511
www.prenticeschool.org

Westmark School
5461 Louise Ave.
Encino, CA 91316
(818) 986-5045
http://westmark.pvt.k12.ca.us

Colorado
Denver Academy
4400 E. Iliff Avenue
Denver, CO 80222
(303) 777-5161
www.denveracademy.org

Havern School
4000 S. Wadsworth Blvd.
Littleton, CO 80123
(303) 986-4587
www.haverncenter.org

Georgia
The Schenck School
282 Mt. Paran Road NW
Atlanta, GA 30327
(404) 252-2591
www.schenck.org

Hawaii
Assets School
School for Gifted and/or
Dyslexic Children
One Ohana Nui Way
Honolulu, HI 96818
(808) 423-1356
www.assets-school.net

Illinois
Brehm Preparatory
  School, Inc.
1245 E. Grand Ave
Carbondale, IL 62901
(618) 457-0371
www.brehm.org

The Hyde Park Day Schools
1375 E. 60th Street
Chicago, IL 60637
  and
1980 Old Willow Road
Northfield, IL 60093
(877) 477-5665
http://hpds.uchicago.edu

Massachusetts
Eagle Hill School
242 Old Petersham Road
Harwick, MA 01037
(413) 477-6000
www.ehs1.org

Landmark School
P.O. Box 227
Pride Crossing, MA 01965
(978) 236-3010
www.landmarkschool.org

Maryland
Jemicy School
301 West Chesapeake Ave.
Towson, MD 21204
(410) 653-2700
www.jemicyschool.org

Norbel School
6135 Old Washington Road
Elkridge, MD 21075
(410) 796-6700
www.norbelschool.org

New Jersey
Cambridge School
100 Straube Center Blvd.
Pennington, NJ 08534
(609) 730-9553
www.thecambridgeschool.org

The Lewis School
53 Bayard Lane
Princeton, NJ 08540
(609) 924-8120
www.lewisschool.org

Purnell School
51 Pottersville Road
Pottersville, NJ 07979
(908) 439-2154
www.purnell.org

New York
The Gow School
2491 Emery Road
South Wales, NY 14139-0085
(716) 652-3450
www.gow.org

New York (continued)
The Kildonan School
425 Morse Hill Road
Amenia, NY 12501
(845) 373-2014
www.dunnabeck.org

North Carolina
Greenhills School
1360 Lyndale Dr.
Winston-Salem, NC 27106
(336) 924-4908
www.greenhillsschool.ws

South Carolina
Trident Academy
1455 Wakendaw Road
Mount Pleasant, SC
29464
(843) 884-7046
www.tridentacademy.com

Tennessee
Bachman Academy
414 Brymer Creek Road
McDonald, TN 37353
(423) 479-4523
www.bachmanacademy.org

Texas
The Shelton School
15720 Hillcrest Ave.
Dallas, TX 75248
(972) 774-1772
www.shelton.org

Vermont
Greenwood School
14 Greenwood Lane
Putney, VT 05346
(802) 387-4545
www.greenwood.org

Pine Ridge School
9505 Williston Rd.
Williston, VT 05495
(802) 434-2161
www.pineridgeschool.com

Learning-Different Testing Facilities and Therapists

FACILITIES

CHADD

Children and Adults with Attention Deficit/Hyperactivity Disorder.
www.chadd.org (Visit the website to find a facility in your area.)

The Shelton Evaluation Center

15720 Hillcrest Avenue
Dallas, TX
(972) 774-1772
www.shelton.org

The Luke Waites Center for Dyslexia and Learning Disorders

Texas Scottish Rite Hospital for Children
2222 Welborn Street
Dallas, TX 75219
(800) 421-1121
www.tsrhc.org

The children's hospital in your area is likely to offer referrals to both diagnosticians and therapists. Find the one nearest you by visiting the National Association of Children's Hospitals and Related Institutions at www.childrenshospitals.net.

For the SPECT imaging procedure, visit www.amenclinics.com or www.clementsclinics.com.

THERAPISTS

The International Multisensory Structured Language Education Council (IMSLEC) accredits quality Multisensory Structured Language Education (MSLE) training courses for teachers and therapists of people with learning differences. You can find out more at www.imslec.org. Certified Academic Language Therapists (C.A.L.T.) can guide your student through his or her remediation process. To find a therapist in your area, visit www.altaread.org.

Sea of Denial Survey

Take this short survey to see where you are with your children regarding the Sea of Denial.

1. My spouse and I talk _____
   about our learning-different child.

   OFTEN (1 point)
   OCCASIONALLY (3 points)
   NEVER (5 points)

2. I and/or my spouse believe that our child will grow out of his/her learning difference.

   TRUE (1 point)
   FALSE (5 points)

3. I and/or my spouse do our own research _____
   to find out the latest scientific findings about learning differences as well as treatment options.

   WEEKLY (1 point)
   MONTHLY (3 points)
   RARELY (5 points)

4. I and/or my spouse talk to our friends _____
   about our child's learning difference.

   OFTEN (1 point)
   OCCASIONALLY (3 points)
   NEVER (5 points)

5. I and/or my spouse feel sad about our child's learning difference.

TRUE (1 points)
FALSE (3 points)

6. Our child is receiving remediation.

TRUE (1 point)
FALSE (5 points)

7. I and/or my spouse try to minimize the severity of our child's learning difference _____ when talking with family and/or friends.

USUALLY (5 points)
SOMETIMES (3 points)
RARELY (1 point)

8. I and/or my spouse blame our child's school for his/her struggles.

TRUE (1 point)
FALSE (5 points)

9. Other people understand our child when he/she speaks.

USUALLY (1 point)
SOMETIMES (3 points)
RARELY (5 points)

10. Our child _____ makes and keeps friends.

USUALLY (1 point)
SOMETIMES (3 points)
RARELY (5 points)

Scoring

10-18 points: Congratulations! You are paddling nicely through the Sea of Denial. Everyone is in the right lifeboat and you are facing the reality of your child's learning difference. Your child will find success on the other side.

18-25 points: Good job! You are dealing with this challenge well. Sometimes you get stuck in a particular current, but you seem to get back on your way easily. Your child will find success as you make your way to the other side.

25-35 points: Rough waters ahead! Watch out . . . you may get blind-sided by one or more of the currents in the Sea of Denial. Take some time to re-evaluate where you are and what you are doing to help your child be successful in mastering his or her learning difference. You are in denial about some aspects of your child's challenges. Find the right lifeboat, climb aboard and move ahead. There is still hope for success.

35-50 points: Look out . . . waterfall ahead! Danger is around the bend if you do not deal with your denial now. Fall back and regroup. Rethink your strategies and decide to put the entire family in the right lifeboats; it is a matter of life and death. Your child's success depends on you making it to the other side.

Couples' Bible Study

WEEK ONE

God created man in the image of himself, in the image of God he created him, male and female he created them.

GENESIS 1:27

Sometimes we forget that God created each of us in His own image. How often do we see our spouse as one who is made in God's image? Meditate on that for a moment; it's a truly overwhelming idea. When was it that we began to believe that it was not that big of a deal?

When we don't keep this fundamental truth at the forefront of our hearts and minds, we become apathetic and complacent with others and ourselves. We become negative and pessimistic about the future. We have a distorted view of who God intended us to be, and inevitably, other areas of our lives become distorted as well. We begin to doubt that God really cares about us, or that our spouse really cares about what we think and feel. We become paralyzed when it's time to make decisions and live in a constant state of confusion.

When we don't live the truth of being God's image-bearers, fear can enter relationships. We may fear the lack of acceptance by others, or a withdrawal of unconditional love from a spouse or child, or being misunderstood.

Take a moment together and ask the following questions.

1. What is my biggest fear? What is our biggest fear?

_____

_____

_____

_____

_____

_____

_____

2. How do I see God's presence in my spouse? Give at least three examples.

_____

_____

_____

_____

_____

_____

_____

If anyone of you thinks of himself as wiser in the ordinary sense of the word, then he must learn to be a fool before he can really be wise (1 Corinthians 3:18-23).

Remember when you were single and you believed that you had it all together? You thought that you were wise beyond your years. You did pretty much whatever you wanted to do whenever you wanted to do it. It was great, right? Then this person entered your life and put a whole new spin on your world. You began to see yourself in a different light, to believe that you would not want to live in this world without this person. You were better with him or her than without him or her. Something great was happening, but exactly what it was was not yet clear; you just knew that it was great.

Then you married and life was great. Yet you soon realized that as strong and wonderful as your love was, you could not be everything to each other. When God is not at the center of the relationship, problems are on the horizon. The first that can arise is the problem of communication. Until they learn how to deeply and effectively communicate, many individuals revert back to their single mentality and live there comfortably, checking in every so often with their spouse to see how everything is going. Unfortunately, when real problems begin to occur within the family (such as your child's learning difference), two married people living as though they are single won't make it.

Ask each other the following questions. Be honest; don't hold back. Before you begin, ask God to be the center of your conversation. Ask Him to help you hear what He wants you to learn.

3. Read Isaiah 29:18 together, then ask each other: Do you really hear what I am saying? On a daily basis? About the children? About our child's learning difference?

   _____

   _____

   _____

   _____

   _____

   _____

   _____

4. What is the best way for me to communicate with you? With our children? With our learning-different child?

_____

_____

_____

_____

_____

5. Tell me about a time when you were truly heard by others. What did that feel like?

_____

_____

_____

_____

_____

6. What can I do to make you feel truly heard in that same way?

_____

_____

_____

_____

_____

7. Tell me about a time when others did not hear what you were trying to say. How did that make you feel?

_____

_____

_____

_____

Surely, you have spoken in my hearing, and I have heard the sound of your words (Job 33:8).

Do not speak in the hearing of a fool, for he will despise the wisdom of your words (Proverbs 23:9).

8. What are some ways we can improve our communication skills with each other? With our children? With others?

_____

_____

_____

_____

_____

_____

WEEK TWO

Whom did he consult for his enlightenment, and who taught him the path of justice, and taught him knowledge, and showed him the way of understanding?

ISAIAH 40:14

The prophet Isaiah tells us in this verse that the path of understanding, knowledge, justice and enlightenment comes from God. Too many times, we believe that we can find these within ourselves. When a child is diagnosed with a learning difference, *pray first* to find out the direction you must take to get the proper help for your child. God is the mighty Healer and the wise Counselor. Pray as a couple to be directed according to His most perfect will, not according to yours.

Discuss, in depth, the following questions.

1. What is our child's learning difference? (Usually there are more than one in the mix, so name them all. Be specific. If you don't know them, decide when you will get testing.)

_____

_____

_____

_____

_____

2. When you first heard that our child had a learning difference, what was your reaction?

_____

_____

_____

_____

_____

3. Do both of us have the knowledge about our child's learning difference and what that means for him/her and our family? If not, how will we educate ourselves as a team?

_____

_____

_____

_____

4. Why do we have a learning-different child? Why did God choose us to parent this child? What qualities do we have that will help him/her?

_____
_____
_____
_____
_____
_____

5. What feelings of disappointment, anger and/or confusion do we have? Do we blame each other for our child's learning difference?

_____
_____
_____
_____
_____

7. Meditate on Matthew 9:27. Do we see God's hand in this situation? How? Give three examples.

_____
_____
_____
_____
_____
_____

WEEK THREE

There is no sound tree that produces rotten fruit, nor again a rotten tree
that produces sound fruit. For every tree can be told by its own fruit:
people do not pick figs from thorns, nor gather grapes from brambles.
A good man draws what is good from the store of goodness in his heart;
a bad man draws what is bad from the store of badness.
For a man's words flow out of what fills his heart.

LUKE 6:43-49

The old saying, "The apple doesn't fall far from the tree," is often true, especially when it comes to learning-different children. As parents, we tend to over-protect them from the hardships of the world, when in fact, because these children tend to have very literal interpretations of life and weak inference-gathering skills, they may not be as wounded as we think.

The truth is they pick up what information we give them. If we explain their learning difference as a bad thing and program them to believe it, they will believe what we say and will find it difficult to achieve anything. Many learning-different children are very bright and learn how to manipulate their parents into skipping remediation or being the center of attention at school or at home. Ironically, parents may actually be showing the child how to perfect these skills through their own behavior.

Ask yourselves if your child is manipulating you. If so, what methods do they use? How do you and your spouse react as a couple to their manipulations? What are the consequences of their manipulations? Answer the questions below and be as honest as possible.

1. How are our actions hindering or helping our child deal with his/her learning difference effectively?

   _____

   _____

   _____

   _____

2. What does our child's future look like right now if we do nothing about his/her learning difference?

   _____

   _____

   _____

   _____

3. What can we do to make our child's future better?

   _____

   _____

   _____

   _____

4. What does our child need to have a successful life? At home? At school? In relationships?

   _____

   _____

   _____

   _____

5. How will we help him/her achieve it? Who will we find to help us help him/her?

_____

_____

_____

_____

_____

_____

WEEK FOUR

*For I am longing to see you either to strengthen you by sharing
a spiritual gift with you, or what is better, to find encouragement
among you from our common faith.*

ROMANS 1:11-12

In this passage, Paul is speaking to the church in Rome, telling them how he longs to see them and share their common bonds of faith. Notice the joy in his tone and how he expresses his anticipation of sharing a spiritual gift.

Married couples have a unique opportunity to daily share spiritual gifts with each other and enhance their common faith. That is why marriage is such a beautiful sacrament. The married life is a living, breathing example of Christ's love here on earth. When we don't activate our spiritual gifts within marriage, we minimize and even degrade what God intended for us. If our marriage is spiritually weak, our families will not withstand the ravages of life.

Answer the following questions and allow God to speak to you about your marriage. Be prepared for miracles.

1. How much time do we give to God in our marriage? How much time do we give Him in our family?

   _____

   _____

   _____

   _____

   _____

   _____

2. What does it look like when we give God time in our marriage and family? What does it look like when we don't give God time in our marriage and family? Be specific.

   _____

   _____

   _____

   _____

   _____

3. How do we show our children how to handle their problems? Is it through prayer? If so, what type of prayer (personal/individual, family, various types of devotion, etc.)? If not, how can we show our family how to pray? How often will we pray as a family? Where will we pray as a family?

   _____

   _____

   _____

   _____

   _____

   _____

4. Do we encourage our children to share their problems with family members? When and where is the best time and place to discuss problems as a family? How often?

_____

_____

_____

_____

_____

_____

5. What can we do to make our marriage better?

_____

_____

_____

_____

_____

_____

6. Read Proverbs 12:4. How much time do we give to just us as a couple? Is it enough? How can we spend more time together?

_____

_____

_____

_____

_____

_____

7. Meditate on 1 Corinthians 7. How healthy is our sex life?
   How can we invite God into the bedroom, too?

   _____

   _____

   _____

   _____

   _____

   _____

8. How can we encourage one another on a daily basis?

   _____

   _____

   _____

   _____

   _____

   _____

WEEK FIVE

*And it is my prayer that your love may abound more and more,
with knowledge and all discernment.*

PHILIPPIANS 1:9

As you have worked your way through this Bible study together
over the last few weeks, you may have noticed the Holy Spirit
beginning to work in your marriage in a new and beautiful way.

This growth will become the new foundation that will help you make better decisions for yourself, each other and your family. Your discernment in future decisions will be clearer. You will be more grounded. Your children will find more peace and success. Why? Because Christ is becoming the center of your marriage.

Now let's look at your learning-different child through Christ's eyes and see what He is calling him or her to do. Go through the questions below as you listen to God's guidance.

1. How is God calling us to parent this unique child? What self-discipline methods does he/she need to be successful? What outside activities will create a well-rounded child?

_____

_____

_____

_____

_____

_____

2. What impact will our marriage have on our children? Our extended family? Our community?

_____

_____

_____

_____

_____

_____

3. Meditate on 1 Thessalonians 5:14-18. Do we encourage our child to be strong through his/her learning difference or do we encourage him/her to stay weak in his/her learning difference? Be specific.

_____

_____

_____

_____

_____

_____

4. What are our goals for our learning-different child for the next six months? One year? Five years?

_____

_____

_____

_____

_____

_____

5. How do we find joy and peace in our everyday life? How do we bring joy and peace to our children? How can we bring more joy and peace to them?

_____

_____

_____

_____

Be joyful always; pray continually; give thanks in all circumstances,
for this is God's will for you in Christ Jesus.

1 THESSALONIANS 5:16-18

Singles' Bible Study

Single parenting has got to be the most difficult and challenging job in our world today, and it's even more complicated when you have a child with a learning difference. Many of the clients that I work with find themselves in this situation. Sadly, they have no one to go through the journey with them, which often causes their feelings of abandonment and fear to climb to new heights. Don't worry! God will be your guide through this winding path, if only you will let Him.

No doubt, you have had to fight some battles to make it this far. It is now time to take off the boxing gloves, and take some time for yourself under the safety of God the Father. That's right; take a deep breath and allow God to give you some direction in the area of your child's learning difference.

"The LORD will call you back as if you were a wife deserted and distressed in spirit—a wife who married young, only to be rejected," says your God. "For a brief moment I abandoned you, but with deep compassion I will bring you back. In a surge of anger, I hid my face from you for a moment, but with everlasting kindness, I will have compassion on you," says the LORD your Redeemer (Isaiah 54:6-8).

1. So often, divorce brings with it a sense of unworthiness to all involved. Choose today not to be a victim anymore. Meditate on the passage above and write about how you believe that you are unworthy to receive love, goodness, kindness or happiness.

   _____

   _____

   _____

   _____

   _____

   _____

2. How might you project the role of a victim or the lie of unworthiness to your child?

   _____

   _____

   _____

   _____

   _____

   _____

3. List three to five positive qualities that you project to your child. How will you make these qualities a habit in your daily life?

   _____

   _____

   _____

   _____

_____
_____
_____

We all want to be loved and accepted and considered as good and holy. But when life throws us a curve ball such as divorce or abandonment, it is not so easy to trust anyone again.

> Such is the destiny of all who forget God; so perishes the hope of the godless. What he trusts in is fragile; what he relies on is a spider's web. He leans on his web, but it gives way; he clings to it, but it does not hold (Job 8:13-15, *NIV*).

4. Meditate on the passage above and ask yourself who you can trust in your daily life.

_____
_____
_____
_____
_____
_____

5. Do you trust God? Why or why not?

_____
_____
_____
_____
_____
_____

6. How will you choose to let Him lead you into a new direction in your life without putting up false walls around you?

_____

_____

_____

_____

_____

_____

As you go on this spiritual journey, do you find yourself falling back into your old ways of doubt and unworthiness? Ask God to pour His precious blood over you to bind anything that is not of Him and place it at the foot of the cross. Have Him replace it with His most perfect will for you in your life.

Let him not deceive himself by trusting what is worthless, for he will get nothing in return (Job 15:31).

WEEK TWO

Finding out that your child has a learning difference can be scary and intimidating. So many questions can run through your mind about circumstances that might have led to his/her challenge. The one thing you must consider is the fact that learning differences are hereditary. And it may not have come from the spouse or the significant other who is now out of your life; you might have a learning difference yourself and may not even know it.

Ask yourself the following questions, and be as truthful as possible.

1. Was school difficult for you as a child? If yes, how was it difficult? (Was it easy or difficult to follow directions? Were you a class clown? Did you fade into the background hoping that no one would call on you? Did you feel lost most of the time in the classroom? Did you make friends easily? Did you keep friends? Was reading difficult? Was math difficult?)

   _____

   _____

   _____

   _____

   _____

   _____

   _____

The LORD will afflict you with madness, blindness and confusion of mind (Deuteronomy 28:28).

As the Scripture above implies, most individuals with learning differences feel that they have been afflicted in a drastic way. As adults they are embarrassed, humiliated and frustrated that many of their school difficulties have spilled over into their adult lives.

2. Look at your own life and ask yourself what type of learning differences you have. If you truly do not have a learning

difference, what learning difference do you believe your child's other parent may be struggling with?

_____

_____

_____

_____

_____

3. How are those differences similar/different from your child's?

_____

_____

_____

_____

_____

4. How would you change your learning experience as a child?

_____

_____

_____

_____

_____

5. What kind of learning experience do you want for your child (homeschool, therapy plus a traditional school experience, public school with whatever assistance they can offer, etc.)?

_____

_____

_____

_____

_____

_____

6. What is holding you back from giving your child everything he/she needs to be successful? (Money? Attitude? Fear? Pride?) Write a prayer asking God to remove any obstacle holding you back from allowing your child to be successful.

_____

_____

_____

_____

_____

WEEK THREE

Don't love differently! What does this mean? A learning-different child knows exactly what it means: Don't put restrictions on your love. Don't make your love conditional. When you get a diagnosis of learning difference for your child, you may feel a moment of guilt or even shame. *How can this be? Nothing ever goes right in my life! What more could go wrong?* When this mindset settles into your daily life, it affects how you perceive your child. It can be very subtle and very dangerous.

Think about how you are treating your child and meditate on the verses below.

Be imitators of God, therefore, as dearly loved children and live a life of love, just as Christ loved us and gave himself up for us as a fragrant offering and sacrifice to God (Ephesians 5:1-2).

1. Now ask yourself, "How am I a fragrant offering to God throughout my day? Do I love my child conditionally or unconditionally?" Be specific.

_____

_____

_____

_____

_____

Our world today is overcome by the "me-factor." No matter who we are, we all have been affected by it. We want everything in our lives to run smoothly. Thinking of the other people in our environments does not often concern us. But as parents, we must put our lives under a microscope to see the areas of our lives where the "me-factor" is eroding our lives with our children, friends and even our relationship with God.

The LORD appeared to us in the past, saying: "I have loved you with an everlasting love; I have drawn you with loving-kindness" (Jeremiah 31:3).

2. What does it mean to be kind? Do you treat your children, friends and coworkers with kindness?

_____

_____

_____

_____

_____

3. Do you have a negative attitude? If so, does it spill over into all areas of your life? Do you want to make an attitude change? How will you go about changing it?

_____

_____

_____

_____

_____

4. Do you treat your learning-different child differently? Why or why not? Do you treat him/her with kindness and respect? Why or why not?

_____

_____

_____

_____

When a wicked man dies, his hope perishes; all he ex-pected from his power comes to nothing (Proverbs 11:7).

5. Reflect on the verse above and ask yourself, "What are my expectations for my learning-different child, academically, socially and spiritually?"

_____

_____

_____

_____

6. What are your child's expectations for him/herself? How can you help to clarify those expectations for your child? How can you give hope to him/her through his/her expectations?

_____

_____

_____

_____

_____

7. How do you see God's presence in your life and in your child's life through the challenge of his/her learning difference?

_____

_____

_____

_____

8. How do you choose to celebrate his/her learning difference?

_____

_____

_____

_____

WEEK FOUR

"Abraham answered, 'God himself will provide the lamb for the burnt offering, my son.' And the two of them went on together" (Genesis 22:8). Isn't our God an awesome God? Here we read that Abraham was willing to offer his only son to God simply because God said so. How many of us do anything because God said so? Perhaps Abraham may have had a few misgivings about it all, but his faith was everything.

God saw the great faith of Abraham and provided exactly what he needed. The ram was conveniently stuck in some nearby bushes. Can you imagine Abraham's relief when God told him to offer the ram instead of his only son? God's provision caused Abraham incredible joy, peace and spiritual strength.

When it comes to our learning-different children, God has everything under control. And He knows how difficult it is to believe that all things will be provided for your child. Like Abraham, you must have a faith that is fearless. Go forward knowing that God will provide whatever you need.

1. What are the provisions God has brought into your life?

   _____

   _____

   _____

   _____

2. What provisions do you need for your learning-different child (educationally, socially, spiritually)?

   _____

   _____

   _____

   _____

3. Write a prayer asking God for the provisions your child needs.

_____

_____

_____

_____

_____

_____

_____

Glossary

ADD—An acronym for Attention Deficit Disorder. Those who have ADD are often inattentive and "spacey." Memory can also be a problem. In severe cases, the individual can't remember what was said just moments ago, and so is unable to follow through on immediate tasks.

ADD medications—Medicines used to balance chemicals within the brain that contribute to the symptoms of AD/HD and related disorders.

ADHD—An acronym for Attention-Deficit Hyperactivity Disorder. Those with ADHD cannot sit still, seem to be driven in all areas of their lives, and can be impulsive socially and physically. They are often aware that their world is spinning out of control, but they don't know how to stop it. This can be true even for very young children.

AD/HD—A convenient written shorthand that refers to both those with ADD and those with ADHD.

Adderall—A stimulant medication used to balance chemicals within the brain, controlling hyperactivity and impulsiveness.

Alphabetic Phonics—A teaching method that evolved directly from Orton-Gillingham that combines all three learning modalities (auditory for spelling, visual for reading, kinesthetic for handwriting). The Instant Spelling Deck for daily 3-minute drills is a set of 98 picture cards used to "unlock" the most probable spelling of the 44 speech sounds. Benchmark Measures geared to the curriculum were added to provide periodic proof of the student's progress in reading, spelling, handwriting and alphabetizing; these guide the teacher's presentation pace and enhance the student's confidence. For more information, contact the Texas Scottish Rite Hospital, 2222 Welborn St., Dallas, TX 75219, 214-559-7425.

Anne Gillingham—In 1936, Gillingham analyzed the structure of language and combined it with Dr. Orton's findings to create the Gillingham Manual.

Aphasia—An acquired language disorder resulting from brain trauma that involves impairments in both comprehension and production. A person with aphasia recognizes an object but cannot understand the written or spoken word for that object.

The Association Method—A multisensory, phonetically based, incremental instruction program for teaching and/or refining oral and written language. Uses auditory, visual, tactile and motor-kinesthetic cues for learning; the Northampton Symbol System for teaching sound-symbol relationships for reading; cursive for writing; a slower temporal rate of speech to provide children more time to process auditorily and more time to observe the speaker's lip movements; and color differentiation to highlight phonemes within words and new concepts in language structures. Each student makes his or her own book as he or she progresses through the Method. For more information, contact the DuBard School for Language Disorders at www.usm.edu/dubard/, University of Southern Mississippi, Box 10035, Hattiesburg, MS 39406-0035, 601-266-5223.

Attention—The ability to attend and hold focus on people and tasks.

Behavior contract—A signed agreement created by parents and their child to make expectations, rewards and consequences clear and concise.

Central Auditory Processing Disorder—A neurological disorder that causes an inability to differentiate, recognize or understand sounds while both the hearing and the intelligence are normal.

Coordination—The ability to manipulate one's body in various environments, which requires all areas of the body to work in sync.

Cultural deprivation—A lack of experiences and stimuli that prepare very young children for education, such as exposure to letters and numbers, music, or drawing and coloring.

Decoding—The ability to recognize letter sounds and their relationship to written words.

Dopamine—A neurotransmitter that affects cognition, motor activity and motivation.

Dysgraphia—A learning difference characterized by difficulty remembering and mastering the sequence of motor movements needed to write letters and/or numbers.

Dyslexia—A neurological disorder that interferes with the acquisition and processing of language. It is hereditary and is imprinted during the fifth to sixth month of gestation. Dyslexia is evident through difficulty with receptive and expressive language, with phonological processing, and with reading, writing, spelling and handwriting.

Edison gene—While there is one gene most often associated with AD/HD (and is the best candidate for the Edison gene), there are others that work with it in different configurations, shading its nuance and power to create the personality of an inventor, explorer or entrepreneur.

Educational deficiency—A lack of educational opportunities, often due to poor socioeconomic background.

Frank brain damage—Neurological impairment due to trauma.

IMSLEC—International Multisensory Structured Language Education Council is an organization that accredits quality multisensory language courses nationwide.

Kussmal—German physician who thought that individuals with reading problems had "word blindness" when seeing the written word.

Language—A spoken and/or written set of symbols used to communicate. Variables such as grammar and spelling make language cohesive and coherent.

Language therapist—A trained professional who remediates children and adults with reading difficulties.

Learning difference—The currently preferred name for learning disabilities such as AD/HD, dyslexia, other disorders of written and oral expression, and dyscalculia.

Linda Mood Bell—The inventor of the Lindamood® Phonemic Sequencing (LiPS) program, designed to stimulate phonemic awareness. Individuals become aware of the mouth actions that produce speech sounds. This awareness becomes a means to verify sounds within words, enabling individuals to become self-correcting in reading, spelling and speech. Bell also pioneered the Visualizing and Verbalizing for Language Comprehension and Thinking (V/V) program, which develops concept imagery beginning with expressive language and extending from a word to imaged paragraphs. For more information, contact Linda Mood Bell Learning Process, www.lblp.com, 416 Higuera, San Luis Obispo, CA 93401, 800-233-1819.

Low mental ability—Below-average on the IQ scale.

Mental Retardation—Below 70 on the IQ scale.

Neural pathways—The paths along which neurotransmitters travel to deliver messages to various parts of the brain.

Neurologist—A medical doctor who diagnoses and treats disorders within the nervous system, especially the brain.

Norepinephrine—A neurotransmitter associated with the fight-or-flight response.

Orton-Gillingham Method—The earliest method devised to teach the learning-different population, which focused on use of all five senses.

Perception—What one understands as reality in one's particular environment.

Perceptual dysfunctions—Learning differences, which are the result of a neurological irregularity leading to difficulties in the areas of visual memory or discrimination, motor skills, and auditory discrimination or memory.

Primary emotional problems—Any emotional problem (such as clinical depression or anxiety) that may interfere with learning and relationships.

Remediation—A process that breaks down language or numbers into smaller segments to improve skills in reading or math. Also includes direct teaching of these skills to raise general competence.

Ritalin—The oldest medication used to treat children and adults with AD/HD. It has been proven to increase the dopamine levels in the brain, helping people with focus and impulse control.

Samuel T. Orton—An American neurologist who, in 1925, proposed the first theory of learning difficulties. Orton realized that these students needed to use all of their senses in order to learn effectively.

SEE—An acronym for Sequential English Education. This is a multisensory, structured approach to teaching reading, writing and spelling to students at risk for or diagnosed with dyslexia or a related language disorder, and is one of only a few programs appropriate for 5- to 6-year-old children. The program initially emphasizes the mastery of the code of the English language, both the alphabetic and phonetic systems. Instruction is 1:1 or small group (1:7) and intensive. Multisensory techniques are integral, such as the use of a memory board (a textured surface of masonite). Comprehension is built starting with decoding word meanings and moving to sentence paraphrasing. For more information, contact The Sequential English Education Training Program at The June Shelton School and Evaluation Center, www.shelton.org, 15720 Hillcrest Ave., Dallas, TX 75248, 214-352-1772.

Sensory deprivation—Lack of stimuli during the early years of child development.

Sensory integration disorder—A neurological disorder that manifests as poor processing in the five senses (hearing, touch, taste, smell and sight). If left untreated, this can mimic AD/HD.

Serotonin—A neurotransmitter that affects mood, emotion, sleep and appetite.

Speech language therapist—A trained professional who works with children and adults with speech difficulties such as stutters, speech delays, cluttered speech and problems in the clarification of language.

SPECT—Single Photo Emission Computed Tomography, a brain scanning technique used by the Amen Clinic to determine what areas of the brain are affected by various learning differences. For more information, go to www.amenclinics.com.

Special education—A provision for students with special needs in the areas of physical or mental disabilities, as well as learning differences. Children who qualify for these services within the public school system have a greater than 16 percent discrepancy between IQ and academic achievement.

The Wilson Method—The Wilson Reading System is a 12-step remedial reading and writing program for individuals with a language-based learning disability. This program is based on Orton-Gillingham philosophy and principles, as well as current phonological coding research. It directly teaches the structure of words in the English language so that students master the coding system for reading and spelling. Unlike other programs that overwhelm the student with rules, the English language is presented in a systematic and cumulative manner so that it is manageable. The Wilson Reading System specifically teaches strategies for decoding and spelling; however, from the beginning steps of the program, it includes oral expressive language development and comprehension. Visualization techniques are used for comprehension. For more information, contact Wilson Language Training, www.wilsonlanguage.com, 175 West Main Street, Millbury, MA 01527-1441, 800-899-8454.

Endnotes

Introduction: My Story

1. Carol Stock Kranowitz, M.A., *The Out-of-Sync Child: Recognizing and Coping with Sensory Processing Disorder* (New York: Perigree Trade, 1998), p. 42.
2. Thom Hartmann, *The Edison Gene: ADHD and the Gift of the Hunter Child* (South Paris, ME: Park Street Press, 2005). *Attention-Deficit Disorder: A Different Perception* (Chelsea, AL: Newleaf Publishing, 1999).
3. Ibid., pp. 4-5.
4. Ibid., p. 4.
5. Betsy Morris, Lisa Munoz, Patricia Neering, "Overcoming Dyslexia," *Fortune* Magazine, May 13, 2002. http://money.cnn.com/magazines/fortune/fortune_archive/2002/05/13/322876/index.htm (accessed June 2008).
6. Paul Orfalea, "Are B Students the Best Managers?" Paul Orfalea's Blog, February 6, 2008. http://paulorfaleasblog.blogspot.com/2008/02/are-b-students-best-managers.html (accessed June 2008).

Chapter 1: What Are Learning Differences?

1. "What Is a Learning Disability?" from the National Center for Learning Disabilities online Parent Center. http://www.ncld.org/content/view/1141/ 456166/ (accessed June 2008).
2. G. F. Eden and L. Moats, "The Role of Neuroscience in the Remediation of Students with Dyslexia," *National Neuroscience*, 2002, pp. 1080-1084.
3. Gayle Zieman, Ph.D., "Nonverbal Learning Disability: The Math and Handwriting Problem," at NDLonline.com. http://www.nldline.com/nld_gayle_zieman_nm.htm (accessed August 2008).
4. Dr. Daniel G. Amen, *Healing ADD: The Breakthrough Program that Allows You to See and Heal the 6 Types of ADD* (New York: Berkley Trade, 2002).
5. I recommend Dr. Hallowell, MD, and John Ratey, MD, *Driven to Distraction: Recognizing and Coping with Attention Deficite Disorder from Childhood Through Adulthood* (New York: Touchstone, 1995) for adults dealing with a recent diagnosis of AD/HD.
6. World Health Organization, "WHO Essential Drugs for Common Psychiatric Disorders in Children." http://www.who.int/entity/selection_medicines/ committees/subcommittee/2/Psychotherapeutic_review.pdf (accessed August 2008).
7. See Hallowell and Ratey, *Driven to Distraction*, for more on this important topic.
8. H. Lee Swanson, Karen R. Harris, Steve Graham, *Handbook of Learning Disabilities* (New York: The Guilford Press, 2003), p. 18.

Chapter 2: God's Purposes in Learning Differences

1. Sirach, from the Apocrypha, *The New English Bible* © The Delegates of Oxford University Press and The Syndics of the Cambridge University Press 1961, 1970, 1989. http://www.goodnewsinc.org/othbooks/sirach.html (accessed June 2008).
2. Adapted from Chris A. Dendy, M.S., *Teenagers with ADD: A Parents Guide* (Bethesda, MD: Woodbine House Publishers, 1995).

Chapter 3: What's a Parent to Do?

1. "Welcome to Holland," ©1987 by Emily Perl Kingsley. All rights reserved.

Chapter 4: Good News About Bad Behavior
1. Sylvia O. Richardson, M.D., "Children at Risk," *Montessori Life*, v. 9, Summer 1997, pp. 26-30.
2. Adapted from "Sensory Integration Dysfunction" from Kid-Power.org. http://www.kid-power.org/sid.html (accessed July 2008).
3. Nancy W. Coffman, MS, CALT, *Shelton School Study Skills*, Appendix (2002), p. 4.
4. Ibid., p. 3.

Chapter 5: Making Sense of Adolescence
1. Adapted from Chris A. Dendy, M.S., *Teenagers with ADD: A Parents Guide* (Bethesda, MD: Woodbine House Publishers, 1995).
2. Ibid.
3. All "Random Polls" culled from "Connecting with Others: Polls" at Schwab Learning's Great Schools™ online resource center, www.greatschools.net.

Chapter 10: Marriage Matters
1. Colleen Alexander-Roberts, *ADHD and Teens: A Parent's Guide to Making It Through the Tough Years: Proven Techniques for Handling Emotional, Academic, and Behavioral Problems* (Boulder, CO: Taylor Trade Publishing, 2001), p. 103.

Chapter 11: Brothers and Sisters: Where Do I Fit In?
1. Abigail Marshall, *The Everything Parent's Guide to Children with Dyslexia: All You Need to Ensure Your Child's Success* (Cincinnati, OH: Adams Media, 2004), p. 103.

About the Author

MAREN ANGELOTTI, M.A.T., is an academic language therapist and AD/HD instructor for both children and adults. She is a frequently requested speaker and a consultant to home-school associations, educational facilities and universities around the country, specializing in dealing with learning differences from a biblical perspective and in implementing effective remediation methods.

Angelotti was born and raised in Southern California. She received bachelor's degrees in Sociology and Theological Studies from Loyola Marymount University in Los Angeles and a master's degree in Teaching for the learning-different student from Dallas Baptist University in Dallas, Texas.

A mother of four, Angelotti first became involved in learning-different education when her daughter was diagnosed with ADD at age 11. In an effort to help her child, she discovered the pain and confusion that many parents go through when trying to help their learning-different children live a normal life.

Angelotti founded Of Different Minds Inc., an organization that provides educational seminars for both teachers and parents, offering them tools to bridge the understanding of the learning-different child and the world around them.

For more information
or to contact the author, visit

www.ofdifferentminds.com